"As someone who has [...] Melissa's transparency, her words of wisdom and the practical tips in *Learning to Roar*. Courage is something everyone can grow but sometimes we just need someone to come alongside us to encourage us and cheer us on. Melissa is that champion." **JJ Gutierrez, Author of Chickening IN-from FEAR to Courageous FAITH**

"Finding the courage to be one's own champion is a struggle many women find themselves in. *Learning to Roar* breathes life into the battle as Melissa unpacks her journey from fear to courage. The insights found in the book will not only offer a view into her relatable road but genuinely inspire you to find that same strength within you." **Darlene Brock, Author of Raising Great Girls**

"As the Founder and Director of Women World Leaders and having an extreme passion to encourage women, this book struck a powerful chord in my heart. The emboldened truths nestled in each chapter resonated with my soul. These helpful nuggets empowered me to press into some courageous steps forward with my own life. It moved me. As a woman of Faith and serving in Gods Kingdom, I understand that courage and strength with faith are a necessity for success. This book provides help. *Learning to Roar* offers a way to strengthen the reader in an encouraging, motivating way with love." **Kimberly Ann Hobbs, Author of Fuel for Life: Abundant Living through Daily Coaching**

"For me the biggest gift in *Learning to Roar* is learning how you too can take steps to cultivate the courage to break the shackles in your own life that are holding you back, find healing from hurts that keep you living smaller than you should. Melissa demonstrates courage on every page." **Lisa K. Baker, PhD, clinical psychologist Co-host of The Cost Is Courage podcast**

"*Learning to Roar* is an authentic look into Melissa's journey toward healing and how courage was cultivated in her own life. Melissa's words speak deeply to the hearts of women by empowering them to live their courageous stories with God as their ultimate Champion. Any Daughter of God will be inspired to open-up, claim her value and be the woman He has made her to be." **Becky Beresford, Author, Speaker, Host of the Brave Women Series**

Learning to
ROAR

Life Lessons on Faith, Courage,
and Female Pride

*Live with courage
always!*

MCD

By Melissa C. Dyer

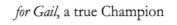

for Gail, a true Champion

Table of Contents

GROUP DISCUSSION GUIDE included.

INTRODUCTION

We stopped what we were doing and looked up. The unfamiliar roar in the distance caused the disturbance. Instinctively, each of us moved in the direction of our cubs first, then those entrusted to our care. We mobilized with synchronicity. Her voice was not just unfamiliar but threatening. Once confident that the cubs were safely tucked away—guarded against the unknown—we began to assume our place in the circle. As a community, we protect our territory. The protective instinct requires no thought, only action. We roar back. Collectively—in unison—our voices are strong.

We were designed for this. Without each other, the pride is more easily overcome by intruders, by danger. Our courage multiplies in community. Without each other, we are vulnerable. We do this defending of our collective territory well; we work together. But that's not always the case with each other. Often, we hesitate to roar at one another. Tentative to express our boundaries. It's here that we pace with tension. The courage of the pride is reliant on the strength of each of its members.

When members of my community invade my shady rest area, I am also threatened. Not necessarily by danger, but of losing my ground. I know the strength of each lioness. But she must find her spot to lay. I will not give in—I roar back to let her know I'm not going anywhere. That's the way it works within the pride: we all need to learn to find our way. Find our shady rest areas.

1

Establishing our territory and roles within the pride lays the groundwork for trust. Defending our territories keeps us fit and strong for the real threats that come our way; for the roar of an outsider that echoes from the distance.

The unfamiliar roar tells me she is approaching our territory. And as we guard and protect the outside of our circle, we need to be sure of this: we—who are within—can trust each other.

Female lions roar not as an act of aggression like their male counterparts—but as an act of protection. The lionesses protect the territory of the pride. Holding their ground is necessary to keep the community thriving. They must be strong for their survival.

They also roar to find each other. A roar from a female lion could be interpreted much the way we use the phrase, "Where are my people?" She calls out to her female companions wanting to keep tabs on their location within the greater landscape of the territory they all occupy. She is clarifying boundaries. As if to say, "I'm here. Where are you?" If you are not in your own space, there might be a spot left unprotected.

The same could be said of us.

Both in community and our relationships with one another, women need to know that if we reveal our sensitivities to our female friends, they will not be exploited. We want to know that we are safe within our circles. We need to be able to trust those closest to us. We learn this through intimacy in our relationships.

That's what this act of roaring is about anyway. In a relationship, we're establishing trust. We're expressing our intentions to those around us. The truth is, a lot of women struggle when the roar— the act of vocalizing our boundaries—comes from within our relationships. It exposes the human pride of both women. It causes both to feel insecure. It raises the question of trust. In this vulnerability, there is a looming question, "Is she safe?"

If our relationships lack intimacy and we respond from a place of insecurity, the relationship can suffer or even break. The tension of discovering where the boundary lines of our territory fall is an art, not a science, within the context of relationships. Since women are innately designed to encourage and support, at some point, when boundaries are crossed the women (involved) will need to be both sensitive and strong. They will need to have courage.

Facing this intimate tension was almost impossible for me for much of my life. When I understood *why* it made all the difference: I had never learned to roar.

This is a book about me taking courageous baby steps in my everyday ordinary life and how that changed me as a person. It's also a book about *you* taking courageous baby steps in *your* everyday ordinary life to find out how you might change as a person. I say *might* because you need to take your baby steps. I'm

3

here to encourage you to take them, but you need to do the work. Change doesn't happen overnight; we all need to start somewhere, and I think encouragement is a good place for us to begin.

Everyone needs encouragement—there are no exceptions. The problem is, not everyone receives it. That's a part of my story; I was in desperate need of encouragement. I needed courage on loan.

Often, our very first step towards courage is taken simply because someone else believes in us. Maybe there was someone in your childhood who was generous with his or her courage? A Champion, if you will—someone who cheered you on and made you feel big, strong, and capable. In those cases, they lent you their courage. That's one of the beautiful things about encouragement: it can flow from others to you, or from you to others, and it nurtures courage.

Courage isn't something you can buy, or make, or inherit but with the borrowed seed of encouragement, it can be nurtured. You can learn to grow it! Throughout the stories I'm going to share with you here, I've learned you can cultivate your courage from opportunities in your everyday ordinary life. Learning this lesson didn't come easily and putting it into action was even harder. But that's what makes this a story about transformation.

For years, I asked God to pull me up out of the low place I was in. I longed for a Champion to appear and save the day by doing the work for me. Spoiler alert: no Champion showed up. Instead, I had to do the hard work. No more sitting around like a damsel in distress feeling sorry for myself or waiting for someone to rescue me, I had to become my own Champion and cultivate my courage.

Like most things in life, becoming a Champion is a process: it takes time, opportunity, and action. But discovering this was possible was life-changing for me, and it's why I am compelled to share my story with you. No matter how discouraged you

I'm here to tell you that you already have what it takes.

are, you don't have to stay there. And please, don't spend any more time waiting for someone to swoop in and save the day for you. I'm here to tell you that you already have what it takes.

Every story has a cast of characters: actors, bystanders, a villain, and a hero or a Champion. While none of the other characters in my story were my Champions, they were all women, and I think that's an important detail to note. Women have been endowed by God to be natural encouragers, yet not all of us know how to use this gift. In my life, I've tried time and time again to assimilate into groups of women—simply looking for encouragement—but I received nothing. I was all dry in the splash zone and completely deflated.

In hindsight, I believe these women had no idea that's what I was looking for and what I needed desperately. At times, I'm not sure I even knew what it was I needed. I just knew I was discouraged and desperate for something different. Something more.

It turns out that God used each of the women in my story like stepping-stones on my journey towards courage, but I want to be clear when I say this is not a book about those people. They provided opportunities for me to grow and learn and become courageous. The truth is, I would not be who I am today without them.

Probably, more importantly, I learned that, while I needed to become my Champion in life, I was not alone on the journey. My story shows me walking this hard road *with* God. Leaning on Him, listening to Him, and, at times, begging Him to make it a little easier for me.

In all of this, here's a thing I've learned about God: He is a Champion, but He will not always swoop in and save the day. Instead, He wants us to develop our courage, to be strong and steady, *like* Him. And one of the ways He accomplishes that is by taking us through—no shortcuts over, under or around—some really hard things. But wherever He takes us, He always promises to come along.

Are you ready to dig deeper with me?

Are you ready to do a little soul searching of your own?

Are you willing to abandon the feeling of discouragement as you take some steps toward courage?

Are you willing to do the hard work of becoming your own Champion?

It won't be easy, but I promise it's worth it. You can start today, right now in your own everyday ordinary life. Cultivating courage only requires one baby step at a time. And you have a Champion in your corner cheering you on each step of the way. Me!

I'm humbled to be able to lend you a little courage as you begin your courageous journey.

Let's get started.

Dear Discouraged,

I've already shared with you my specific area of discouragement; I had never learned to roar. The ability to speak up for myself and express when my feelings had been hurt seemed beyond my capability. I lacked the courage. That's what the feeling of discouragement reveals, a lack of courage. But don't confuse lack with non-existence. It's there, deep within you.

That's why I'm using the illustration of a seed as a way to help you understand my story. Because the growth was internal, not external. Courage is an inside job. When the transformation from discouraged to encouraged is happening, only you will know. No one knew this transformation was happening inside of me either. But eventually, there will be enough growth to break through the hiddenness for others to see.

However, some of us need to see examples to learn. There were phases of my journey where I needed a vision for what could be; I had to see some things for myself. And once I had a vision, I needed to take some action. I wholeheartedly believe the breakthrough lies in taking action.

These letters are invitations along the way for you to take action and experience your own breakthrough in three key areas: faith, growth, and community. So, pay attention. Look for them at the end of each chapter in Part Two of the book.

Taking steps in these areas will require courage. Use what you've already got, remember you're growing more!

I believe in you, Melissa

PART ONE

The need to change.

CHAPTER ONE

You may not control all the events that happen to you, but you can decide not to be reduced by them.

Maya Angelou

Everyone adored the kitchen in my last house, myself included. I couldn't take any credit for it as the previous owner had completed all the custom renovations. However, I often shamelessly accepted the praise. It was small by most standards, as was the rest of our home, but it had a few upscale features I enjoyed. And truly, most of the guests we invited into our home only noticed the décor. The best thing about that kitchen was the life we lived within its walls. It was the page on which the intimate story of our family had been written, a page full of family memories. Heart memories.

Memories like the rainy day we spent crowded in that tiny space, our family of four plus a couple we had supported and loved for years—immigrants we mentored and cherished and helped to become American citizens. All six of us covered in flour, hot from the steam of boiling water on the stove; each of us crimping the edges of tiny perogies until our fingers were sore.

Memories of hundreds of Christmas cookies carefully fashioned on granite counters by little hands. It was where my children

13

spent hours studying arithmetic, grammar, and science. Homeschool co-ops gathered. Birthday candles blown out. It was a happy place that held the stories of our family life. And, because of that, it was more than a kitchen to me; it was my treasure box. It was in this space where I displayed my beloved cookbooks, collection of seashells, and scented candles. It was the place in which I was the most vulnerable and the least guarded.

And maybe, that's why—when a very unexpected thing happened to me in my kitchen—it sullied all the happy memories that kitchen held and created a memory I don't treasure. A memory that stings.

She was invited.

I had opened up not only my home to her and her family, but my life too, with all of its imperfections. Isn't that what we are called to do as Christians? Open up our lives to one another? Love one another?

Of course, with all of this *invitation to openness* comes the turbulent reality that we all have a story, and within those stories, we carry our pain and brokenness. Tender spots that we don't always know what to do with. If we are courageous enough to look those tender spots in the eye and work through the pain they cause, they might reveal to us opportunities for growth and healing. But more often than not, most people learn to protect themselves—their tender spots—by setting formal boundaries, and sometimes by erecting walls.

On this particular evening, I expected our guests to bring their formality with them.

In hindsight, I can see how all the disarming hospitality I had previously extended to this woman and her family could have led to the confusion. Why would she assume that this night would be any different than the numerous others she had spent with us in our home? She probably expected a casual gathering similar to others we had shared. But, on this night, I had conceived a special celebration and expected all the guests to follow the host's lead. I shouldn't have assumed.

It was a memorable occasion and, with great intention, I planned for it to be just that. It was my husband's birthday and I had invited about a half a dozen families to celebrate with us. Attention to detail was the order of the day. I carefully selected the menu of Greek cuisine: a mixed grill of marinated shrimp, chicken, and beef, dressed in fresh squeezed lemon juice and perfectly arranged over a bed of seasoned orzo. On the side was a huge crudité of vegetables with several varieties of Mediterranean hummus. Candles flickered throughout the dining room and back yard, white linens draped the tabletops, and soft music played in the background. It. Was. Perfect. One by one our friends arrived, and our home was filled with rich conversation and companionship. The atmosphere was everything I had hoped for in my planning.

Until her sassy words pierced my bubble of perfection.

After welcoming her family into our home and providing some space for them to join the rhythm of casual mingling in the back yard, she returned to find me, in my kitchen. She sauntered (a skill I have come to appreciate but have yet to acquire) in without so much as a warning and asserted boldly, "I have a birthday blessing I've prepared for the guest of honor." I was soon to find out that she meant a speech. "I'd like you to call everyone in later so they can hear it." And, as abruptly as Sassy had arrived, she turned back around and walked out, slowly melting into the crowd gathered in our backyard. I could almost envision the swing of her tail.

It wasn't the words that wounded me. It was the interaction. Stunned, I stood there alone in my fragility, like a broken piece of jewelry, desperately in need of mending, tucked away in my treasure box. She, on the other hand, was clueless.

Immobilized by her words, my mind desperately cast about for a way to explain to me what had just taken place. A million emotions began to surge through my body with a power of their own. *"Don't give in, don't cry,"* I told myself. My acute vulnerability and my instinct toward self-preservation wrestled for control of my expression. Thankfully, self-preservation won, and I was able to mask the hurricane brewing within me. But the truth is, I was in pain.

It was right here, where my story *should have* played out differently.

My husband and I had taken a bold leap a few years earlier to relocate our family to a new state, to follow a dream. As a family, we were living an exciting story. But, instead of feeling emboldened by our bravery and fulfilled in our new place, I felt small. I had clung to my feelings of failure for so long that deep discouragement had set in. Everything in my life felt small; when you have low self-esteem everything around you has a scaled vantage point, except you. I continued to blame myself for the mistakes we had made and didn't have the encouragement I needed to help build me up.

There are many things I *should have* done in my kitchen that night: speaking up, calmly using my voice to say no to her assertion, being my own Champion. I *should have* been courageous enough to say, "That doesn't fit with how I've planned the evening but thank you for offering."

Regretfully, I felt small and I lacked courage. Instead, I stood there, feeling low. And hurt. And, without a Champion in sight, I lingered in that place for way too long.

Of course, her offense wasn't morally, ethically, or technically wrong. But my feelings were hurt, and her actions were flat out unacceptable to me. Isn't that the root of most tension anyway, a difference in perspective? From my perspective she violated a personal boundary by assuming that a guest could add to the plan for the evening.

To tell you the truth, I wasn't even aware that I had this personal boundary until the incident. All I knew at the moment was somehow my peaceful, planned-out program for the evening had been hi-jacked. She one-upped me and I was completely caught off-guard and ill-equipped to address this unexpected turn of events. I felt powerless and angry. But my anger was mostly directed inward at my inability to speak up. *Why didn't I respond?*

At the time, I assumed she did it because she had a low opinion of me. I assumed she viewed me as small as I viewed myself. But I've learned enough in the years since that the whole situation wasn't really about her actions at all. Rather, my inaction. It was about how I viewed myself. Her actions simply highlighted an area of my life where I clearly had some work to do. The interaction led me to an opportunity to cultivate some courage in an area where I needed it to grow.

To this day, I struggle to glean any happy memories from that evening; negative emotions have a way of scorching our ability to remember the good. Dealing with my emotions that night needed to wait until the end of the evening. I remained physically present for the hours that followed the kitchen incident, but my mind and emotions had retreated. In the privacy of my head, they had been in discourse, building their case until they had an opportunity to be heard.

As my husband gently closed the front door behind the last departing guest of the night, he had no idea what was about to be unleashed. I was ready to take off the mask I had worn all evening and expose my pain; the waiting had been insufferable. A slew of words, tears, and justifications poured out uncontrollably. He was confused. Feeling the need to explain my point of view added insult to the injury. The night ended poorly, and it certainly wasn't what I had envisioned for his birthday party. I was crushed; the beautiful evening I planned was tainted.

For hours, days, and weeks after the party, I picked up the verbal debris over and over again, one piece at a time. Examining each word like pieces of a puzzle attempting to put the whole incident in perspective. Each time, I was left with one looming question: *Why hadn't I been able to respond?* I just silently let it happen.

As I went over it time and time again in my head, there was no hiding that this was a recurring theme in my life. The inability to respond or to speak up when someone violates my boundaries was something all too familiar. I could move my family on a leap of faith to start a new life in another state, but I couldn't speak up for myself. I lacked courage, especially in this area. And, after some serious self-reflection, I knew that if I didn't work through this, I would find myself stuck in the role of powerless victim of my own life, instead of the extraordinary everyday hero I aspire to be. A Champion. *That single realization was the beginning of my journey.*

> I knew that if I didn't work through this, I would find myself stuck in the role of powerless victim of my own life, instead of the extraordinary everyday hero I aspire to be.

Our society desperately needs courageous humans. I'm not referring to more people who will jump out of a plane while recording it live for social media. I mean humans who are willing to do something hard and meaningful, something that holds value over a long time. Humans who are willing to get uncomfortable, not just for a thrill or for attention, but for something or someone worth getting uncomfortable for.

Our generation needs extraordinary women—like you and me—out in the world living extraordinary lives. Our generation needs strong and courageous women holding up every pillar of our society at every level.

I'm saddened that what our society views as courage today is not the courage of previous generations. Instead, it has been confused with success, with celebrity, with being spectacular. Like other pressures that this generation puts on progress, it has succeeded in shortcutting courage. But the truth is, courage can't be rushed. You can't take shortcuts to a courageous life. It needs to be cultivated—and it's an inside job. That was where I needed to start and it's where you'll need to begin also.

That's why I'm offering you a glimpse at the road I've already traveled. Because I know how hard it is to take those first tentative, awkward steps. And I want you to know that although the journey won't be easy, it will be worth it. You are going to have

> You can't take shortcuts to a courageous life.

to do the hard work of cultivating your courage, but you won't be walking this road alone. I'll be cheering you on every step of the way, starting with the baby ones. Even baby steps will set you (and me) on a path to reach our everyday extraordinary dreams that require courage.

Before we begin, we both need to commit. You can commit to doing the hard work toward becoming the most courageous version of you. And I'll commit to sharing the story of my baby steps towards courage and providing you with courage on loan that you'll need for the journey.

As we travel this road together, you'll probably see that you and I are not that different. Our ordinary lives may have similarities: families that we love, friends we support and enjoy, and a desire to contribute to and serve our communities. We long to be living vessels from which we pour into those around us. We likely both want our everyday ordinary lives to have extraordinary meaning. Our destinations may be different, but the journey is essentially the same.

It is a virtuous aspiration to want our lives to have great meaning. I'm not saying our lives don't have meaning just as they are, but for you and me, that's not enough. We're looking to leave something extra-ordinary behind, to leave a deeper impression on the world around us. We want a shred of our existence to outlive us.

And this will never happen if we are stuck in discouragement.

Before I could even start on this journey, I had a choice to make. I could change nothing and stay stuck in a place of discouragement, riddled with low self-esteem. Or, I could choose to move toward becoming the strong and courageous woman God created me to be. Once I decided that I could no longer accept the status quo, only then could I take my first tentative steps toward change, change that would come in three movements.

Step One was to become self-aware. Accepting that my view of myself, both in mindset and perspective, would never get me where I wanted to go, nor would it help me become who I wanted to be (or who I believe God wanted me to be).

Step Two was identifying the patterns of cowardly behavior that had grown out of that mindset. I needed to realign my way of thinking. A new mindset would yield new behavior. This step took the longest. Since I had confused other people's estimation of my value with my actual value, I had learned to treat myself poorly. I needed to unlearn certain behaviors like beating myself up for making mistakes.

Step Three was taking action. Cultivating is the act of preparing the soil for growth. And so, if I was going to cultivate some courage in my life, I needed to pull some serious weeds that had grown throughout my lifetime. Starting with the weed that asserted I wasn't worth the effort.

I'm not going to sugarcoat this for you, it was painful. But with most pain, when processed all the way, I experienced growth and healing.

And that's why I'm so passionate about sharing my story with you. Because who doesn't want to be healed?

Your root of discouragement may not be planted in the soil of low self-esteem, but you may struggle with something else, like facing your fears, processing your pain, or the inability to overcome adversity. Maybe you're having a hard time finding clarity around what you're passionate about which leaves you feeling unfulfilled and purposeless? All of these different roots of discouragement require courage to conquer them. By cultivating courage in the area where we most need it, we're doing the work of preparing the soil of our lives to grow some amazing things.

CHAPTER TWO

Love yourself first and everything else falls into line. You really have to love yourself to get anything done in this world.

Lucille Ball

After the kitchen incident I knew I had to look for some weeds. While some might call it *"soul searching,"* and others may refer to it as *"self-discovery,"* I'm not fancy. For me, it was weeding. It required me to take an unpleasant walk down memory lane in search of understanding why I lacked courage in this area. It meant digging up the memories that only find their way into my mental feed by way of triggers, the ones that are buried deep. And, as I dug, there was one memory in particular that surfaced vividly.

I was heading into adolescence and my life had been upset in just about every conceivable way. My parents had divorced two years earlier and any stability I once had was gone. The transience in my life reached a climax when my mother sent me half-way across the country to live in another state with my grandmother and two aunts, whom I barely knew. I felt abandoned and neglected, the opposite of valued. In short, my life had been turned upside down. Although this season of transition would only last a few months, it served me well in one way: exposing behaviors in me that I may otherwise have never discovered.

As humans, our responses to our environment and the people around us can significantly impact who we become. If the environment is healthy, the habits and behaviors we develop are usually positive. But when the environment is toxic, a lot of negative things can take root and start to grow. A time of disconnecting from the people in your life and your familiar surroundings can flush your system of external influences. Moving across the country—away from the unstable home life I was in—allowed me some breathing room to look objectively at the toll those circumstances had taken on me. It was during this season of uprooting and transplanting that I first discovered my cowardly behavior.

Even though we were both in the sixth grade, she seemed like a giant to me. This perspective wasn't only due to my low self-esteem; she was intimidating in stature and attitude. Just walking down the halls of our junior high would send students to either side of the locker-lined walls as if she had parted the Red Sea. There's no gentle way of phrasing it: she was the school bully.

As I walked into the girls' locker room, I stumbled right into the thick of it. There she was, all five feet and then some, leaning over a classmate to incite fear. The girl she was threatening was scrawny; it was an unfair match up, to say the least.

The school I attended was living up to its reputation for being tough and every day held tense moments. To that end, I probably shouldn't have been so surprised at what I had walked into. I was, however, surprised by my response to it.

I can only imagine it was reflex and adrenaline that moved me to step into the conflict. Before I could even think about what I was doing, I had become a human barrier between Bully and Scrawny. All three of us were startled by my interference. But it had the desired effect; instead of continuing to threaten Scrawny, Bully did quite the opposite, she recoiled quickly. In the uncomfortable pause that followed, I found myself silently pleading for a teacher to walk into the locker room and save us. Even then, I was looking for a Champion. But no one showed up.

> Even then, I was looking for a Champion. But no one showed up.

Still standing nearby, Bully was undoubtedly considering her next move because she promptly changed targets and lobbed a verbal grenade across the room in my direction. *"You just wait, this isn't over."*

Scrawny and I were both relieved that her attack ended up being verbal, at least for the moment. As we watched her exit the locker room, we each sat, paralyzed, accompanied only by the deafening sound of our racing hearts. Eventually, we went back to class and there was nothing left to do but wait for the promised retaliation. An icky feeling of insecurity traveled around with me for the rest of the day. I was grateful when the bell rang, and I headed toward the bus line—I was ready to get home.

I grabbed my seat early, being sure to get by the window. I was emotionally exhausted and as I leaned gently against the pane, I rehashed the whole ordeal in my mind, word by word, over and over. This must be how I had missed her boarding my bus.

My stop was near the end of the route and as the big yellow bus rounded the last corner and slowed to its destination, daylight was beginning to fade. As it halted, the driver leaned over to pull the hand lever opening the squeaky doors. I sighed, grabbed my backpack and stack of three-ring binders, and made my way to the front. I didn't hear her exiting the bus behind me.

She waited just long enough for the bus driver to lose sight of us before she made her move, a simple syllable: "Hey!"

The sound of her voice made me stop dead in my tracks; I couldn't believe she had followed me home. "Why don't you show me how tough you are now," she incited again. I think they refer to these as "fighting words." She continued her verbal provocations as I stood there, frozen. Her final attempt to pull me into the fight was grabbing the binders I held and heaving them onto the sidewalk with her thick paw. Still, I remained paralyzed and silently took it. *Where was the girl who stood up for Scrawny just hours earlier, I wondered?*

Eventually, she became bored with me just standing there. And as she turned to leave, she threw one final dagger my way,

"Guess you're not that brave after all." Devastatingly, it was true. *Where was that brave girl when I needed her?*

I watched her walk away, fading towards the horizon, until her silhouette was nearly gone. By this time, the streetlights were lit, and I stood there alone, in the dusk, on the street corner, ashamed. As tears rolled down my cheeks and fell to the sidewalk, I knelt to gather my belongings and started toward home, head hung.

It was in this memory that I isolated my weed. The painful reality was that I had behaved this way for years. I was able to speak up for someone else but unable to do it for myself. I was just as stunned by my lack of a response as I was over the whole attack, and the shame of that realization buried itself deep within me, like a seed that began to germinate and grow.

Memories like these—the hard, ugly ones—can bury themselves within us, especially if we don't take the time to process them. In a healthy place, what I had felt and labeled as shame should have been processed as a simple lack of experience. At that stage in my life, I had been given no training in conflict resolution or even working through a simple disagreement, and I certainly had not learned how to use my voice to express myself. I know now that all of these things can be learned, just like courage can be cultivated, by anyone, at any stage of life. This is what it means to become your own Champion.

After the kitchen incident—I knew I needed to critically look at the weeds of discouragement in my life and start tugging— digging for the root. I had to ask some hard questions of myself, the most pressing being, *where did the courageous girl who stood up for Scrawny go when push came to shove?*

It was my momentary display of courage, followed by the lack thereof, that had me perplexed. As much as it pained me to acknowledge my weakness, it was a necessary stop on the journey; I had to know where I was so I could take a baby step leading in the direction I wanted to go. And, after sifting through decades of memories that had some element of conflict, I began to see a pattern.

> As much as it pained me to acknowledge my weakness, it was a necessary stop on the journey; I had to know where I was so I could take a baby step leading in the direction I wanted to go.

When it came to defending someone else, courage prevailed, but when it came to defending myself, it was nowhere to be found. This particular memory showcased the radical difference between the two circumstances. Clearly, I had fallen short when I should have spoken up. There's that *should have* again— you see, when I fell short in my own eyes, my automatic response was harsh judgment and self-shaming. Over time, the toll that shame and judgment took on me was devastating. It left me with a lifetime supply of *should haves.*

Perhaps, if I had Champions, they may have helped me balance the scales. They might have been able to offer perspective and encouragement, lending me the weight of their strength. But, at the time, I had no Champions and bore the full weight of all my perceived failures.

It's said that if we don't know what the problem is, we can't work toward a solution. But once we know, we can't remain in blissful ignorance anymore. Through the process of re-examining this memory, I realized that my perceived lack of worth was at the center of my low self-esteem and my inability to defend myself. After all, it stood to reason that if I valued myself, then protecting myself would come naturally; I certainly had no problems coming to the aid of someone else.

Much like weeds, negative behavior patterns are hard to kill, they must be pulled at the root. For me, I desperately needed to shift from my instinct to run away or be paralyzed by conflict and, instead, learn how to address confrontation head on. Learning how to use my voice and speak up for myself was a skill I had yet to develop. Once I had identified the root of my discouragement, I knew that if I wanted to change, I would have to overcome my fear of conflict. And if I wanted to change, a decision was upon me: I had to decide I was worth the effort that would be required of me to do it.

Find the root of the weed, then pull it out.

I knew the journey would not be an easy one, but I was worth it.

31

CHAPTER THREE

Turn your wounds into wisdom.

Oprah Winfrey

I was 19 and found myself in yet another new environment.

My heart desired to be a full-time student, but a series of economic disappointments had thrust me into the working world instead. Once again, my needs and desires had been deprioritized and I was expected to rebound without support. The commitment to a 40-hour work week was a huge adjustment and everything seemed overwhelming to me. Emotionally, I was in a raw and vulnerable place. The thought of my peers enjoying the freedom of transitioning from class to class across the expansive campus of my town's historic university while I remained caged in the confines of florescent lighting amplified my discouragement.

> I hoped this temporary discomfort would be just another step on my courageous journey.

Despite it all, the tumultuous years of my childhood made me a veteran of change and so I hoped this temporary discomfort would be just another step on my courageous journey. While I didn't like the transition into the workforce, it did allow me to tap into an area of my courage that was well-conditioned: *the ability to stretch beyond my comfort zone.*

To that end, I threw myself into my work and developing that particular area of my courage even more. The job was the perfect opportunity to stretch myself: and I did! There was so much to learn. I suspected my coworkers were exhausted by my endless questioning and novice mistakes, but if they felt that way, they didn't let it show. For the most part, the women I worked with were kind and patient with me. It felt more like a family, than an office, albeit a dysfunctional family. It was very much as I envision living in a house full of sisters might be.

As you can imagine, the situation had both pros and cons.

I had been tasked with the hefty responsibility of planning a luxurious retreat for a group of company managers. It was quite the ask of this 19-year-old. It would be a long weekend in the "Big Apple" that would deliver the best that the city had to offer, and it was on me to make the arrangements.

After laying some groundwork via phone and fax (yes faxing was the thing in those days), one of my more senior coworkers and I headed to the city to look at our hotel options in person. She knew New York like the back of her hand and after the 3-hour train ride there, we wandered the busy streets and I enjoyed her lead. I felt safe and secure as she showed me the ropes—it was an experience like no other. Until we arrived at our first appointment.

I had arranged to meet the group sales coordinators at the two hotels we were considering for our retreat: The Plaza and the Waldorf Astoria. And, I would be meeting them on my own. I can't imagine what they thought when I showed up for the meetings—this 19-year-old dressed up in a suit, pretending to be an adult. To say I was uncomfortable was an understatement. I felt like I had no business being there and no clue of how to fake my way as if I did.

> To say I was uncomfortable was an understatement.

The truth was, I needed the help of my savvy coworker several times during those meetings. (Oh, how text messaging would have come in handy that day!) It wasn't long before I caved. I needed back-up and had no choice but to call Savvy in to my appointments. Even with my lack of experience, I knew it was more important to be a little awkward and somewhat embarrassed than to fake my way through the meeting and be stuck making a mistake that would be hard to fix.

While I still vividly remember the bruise to my pride that day, so many other positive details about the experience are etched into my memory: the sparkle of the chandeliers, the polished brass of the elevator walls, and the tufted velvet seating in the hotel lobbies. I learned a lot from my coworker that day—she imparted some street smarts I needed and would use to navigate city life in the future—and we had some fun. Lunch at the Bull and Bear, dinner at Sardis and a visit to the shoe department at Macy's completed our trip. It was time to return to work.

Back in our dysfunctional family office environment, my relationship with Savvy shifted a bit and, over time, our roles resembled sisters more than mentor and mentee. I no longer needed a chaperone, and with a different set of skills than she had displayed on our trip to the city, Savvy was showing me the ropes of sibling rivalry.

One day, we found ourselves in a bit of a verbal back and forth over what was, really, nothing more than a miscommunication. But we were hashing it out a bit, fangs exposed.

Until the office manager arrived, clearly stressed out.

"I don't need the two of you acting like this," she snapped, in a tone that matched her stress level. "You should both just shut up and get over it." Her words were direct and harsh. The power of her roar caused me to shudder.

At the time, she was dealing with a company crisis and was close to breaking. Our little spat seemed to be her tipping point. When I think back on it now—with some experience under my belt— I am sympathetic; I know how stress perverts our personalities. But at the time, her words threw me into a state of panic. Instantly, I was speechless and felt naked in my vulnerability. The insecurity left me threatened as I cowered in place.

The two women standing in the doorway to my office were none the wiser. To the more experienced and confident leaders in our office family, her outburst was considered acceptable behavior. But I didn't know that, and I was both hurt and offended.

And as I had conditioned myself to do, I bottled up all my feelings and looked for a place to run. My eyes scanned my surroundings for an exit. The wall clock that hung just above the doorway I was facing said it was close to noon and I was relieved. I would only need to hold onto all that pain for a few minutes until I could leave for my lunch break.

As the clock hand landed on twelve, I quickly made my way to the office lobby and headed out the door, holding back tears. I walked across the parking lot, the effort it took to

> And as I had conditioned myself to do, I bottled up all my feelings and looked for a place to run.

maintain my composure was like trying to cover a crack in the Hoover Dam with my hands. And just when I was safely in my VW Golf, the tears breached, and the dam let loose a torrent of emotion.

With wet cheeks, I made the quick drive to the university where my college boyfriend was waiting and I buried my head in his chest, trying desperately to regroup. Once the sobbing was finished, he became the only witness in the courtroom that day as I played judge and jury, rehashing the whole scene to him, including justifying my flight from the office.

He knew how close I had grown with my older co-workers and didn't want me to do something I would regret. And, I was looking forward to returning to New York in a few months to supervise the trip with the other guests. Sadly, however, that never happened. I didn't attend the once-in-a-lifetime trip I had planned. Chicago, the Musical on Broadway. Eating at Tavern on the Green. Riding in a horse-drawn carriage through Central Park. I missed out on all of it due to a lack of courage.

Which was exactly my problem. When faced with direct conflict, we only have a few options; stand firm and face the opposition, freeze, or flee. And, in that circumstance—feeling caught off guard and vulnerable—I fled. The pattern of not standing up for myself that was established in my childhood was still an issue as a young adult. Before my lunch break had even ended, I made the most cowardly series of decisions available to me and within minutes of arriving back at my desk, I submitted my letter of resignation. My colleagues were in utter disbelief, unaware that our shared experience had been so polarized.

> When faced with direct conflict, we only have a few options; stand firm and face the opposition, freeze, or flee.

To this day, the memory of those events still makes me feel nauseated.

Of course, I know now that all I needed to do was speak up; to say politely, but with conviction: "Excuse me, I'm not okay with how you just spoke to me." All I needed to do was stand up for myself, but I didn't. Instead, my low self-esteem and lack of courage prevailed, and I quit.

This was exactly the kind of situation where my coworkers, Savvy included, would have had endless encouragement and helpful advice for me. I *should have* cried on their shoulders; we *should have* eaten something chocolate and I *should have* left work that Friday with wind in my sails. Instead, I ran away and ended up feeling alone and crushed. I had thrown away the support and encouragement I longed for simply because my feelings were hurt.

When it came to face-to-face conflict, I would find myself stuck in this cycle for years. That missed opportunity was one of the biggest regrets I carried into my adult years, but, at the same time, it was also the circumstance that planted the small seed of courage I needed to grow.

In the wake of this regret, came the slow realization that I had some patterns I needed to break. To become the confident woman I longed to be and others perceived that I was, I would need to be able to handle conflict in a healthy way, without running away. I needed to grow my courage to become a Champion—not just for others, but for myself.

> When it came to face-to-face conflict, I would find myself stuck in this cycle for years.

Life would soon take me on a very long journey to learn this lesson.

When I look back on this experience, I can see a few things that, for a long time, remained unclear to me. In addition to the slow dawning of awareness around my conflict-avoiding tendencies, I also began to recognize the tension that often exists within female relationships.

The lessons learned in that office full of sisters were many and complex. Women have a deep need for companionship and friendship which—in an ideal world—is complemented by the natural need to give and receive encouragement within those relationships. The very thing we desire from each other is the very thing we must offer liberally: encouragement.

> The very thing we desire from each other is the very thing we must offer liberally: encouragement.

But what happens when the other women in your life are viewed as competition? Suddenly, it's more difficult to offer genuine encouragement and support, because we feel threatened by their success. Instead of celebrating, we compare. Instead of being happy for them, we become jealous, uncomfortable, discouraged.

But the truth of the matter is counterintuitive. The way to get the most out of your relationships with other women is to encourage them and champion their successes. The more you sow the seed of encouragement, the more encouragement there will be for you to borrow when you need it. It can become a beautiful harvest of courage. But finding a community of women invested in championing each other can be a challenge.

In many ways, I had found that unique quality in my office family. But in my lack of experience and my lack of courage, I didn't even give them a chance. I ran away from the very thing I needed most.

Over the next decade, as my self-awareness grew, I made the brave decision to learn from this experience. I realized that I lost that community—ran away from it— because I lacked courage. The recognition that I would have to change felt like a small seed had planted itself deep within me, over time it would take root.

I ran away from the very thing I needed most.

And those were the roots that needed to occupy the soil of my life. Good roots. Roots that refused to share space with the weeds. It would be time to pull those weeds of running away once and for all. I didn't know it at the time, but God was about to show up in a big way.

Not to pull the weeds for me, but to pull the weeds through me.

PART TWO

*A vision for what
could be.*

CHAPTER FOUR

Pain nourishes courage. You can't be brave if you've only had wonderful things happen to you.

Mary Tyler Moore

I was definitely standing, not sitting.

I am certain of this because I remember the distance my tears traveled before they gently absorbed into the teal carpet blanketing the church sanctuary floor. There were a lot of tears. As I silently sobbed, I led myself through my own prayer of sorts.

"God, I'm really messed up. Please fix me."

That was the simple, yet sufficient, cry of my heart. I was so broken.

When people are devalued by others, it doesn't take long until they begin to underestimate their worth. Over time, if left unchecked, it can become part of their identity. If we don't value ourselves, we'll treat ourselves accordingly. And, ultimately, we will break.

45

That was where I was at: broken. I needed some serious fixing. It was only a few, short years after the office incident and, true to who He is, God showed up. It's hard to describe what I felt at that moment, as I prayed. Release, maybe? Something in me had been freed from the heavy work of trying to hold myself together. My tears signaled that there was something new going on inside me; something more than me. The strange thing was, as I left the comfort of the church service that morning, aware that the world outside the doors was exactly the same as I had left it just an hour or so before, I knew I had changed. I was still broken but, somehow, changed.

> Something in me had been freed from the heavy work of trying to hold myself together.

A broken person generally isn't strong enough to make fundamental changes on his or her own. And so, the option of putting the burden of brokenness squarely on someone else to provide the strength, wisdom, and resources to fix them becomes highly appealing. For me, at that moment in church, I firmly grasped hold of a message that told me that "Jesus saves," because I was in a pit of discouragement and desperate to be pulled up and out of my own mess.

I assumed this God named Jesus was going to swoop in and save the day for me. I was convinced He would be my Champion. And, while those things are true—in a manner of speaking—Boy! Did I misunderstand the message!

I wonder if anyone would come to a church service if this was the "good news" that was flowing from the pulpit:

"Jesus is inviting you into eternal life and offering forgiveness for your sins so that you can be in a relationship with the living God of Creation. Only Jesus can extend this invitation to you. If you choose to receive this new and eternal life, here's what you can expect: life as you know it will be full of challenges and struggles – but Jesus will be with you through it all. A mission impossible of sorts. And as He is with you through it, He intends to build you up, make you strong, increase your endurance for pain. Experiencing the same pain, He endured to extend this invitation to you is His plan. The God of Creation is re-creating you, reworking your brokenness, your mess, to look like Jesus. **It won't be easy, but it will be worth it."**

I'm not sure how many people would say, "Yes, count me in!" to a message that communicates so clearly, "This will be hard."

It's a good thing we don't hear how hard it will be at the beginning—I'm convinced that's God's grace in action. He doesn't want us to shrink back from what is best for our lives, He doesn't want us to quit. Instead, He leads us little by little out of our pit, careful not to overwhelm our fragile nature. The process is God's gracious kindness toward us.

Fixing broken people is a process. Fits and starts come with the territory.

Following my teary moment at church, and after going it alone for a few weeks, I knew I needed some human guidance on my spiritual journey. Initially, I had employed a simple strategy of just trying to keep myself out of trouble. I filled my time doing "good things" hoping that the temptation to do "bad things" would stay sidelined. It worked for a while, but I wasn't growing and didn't know how to tell Jesus that I needed him to speed things along for me.

I sought out a female member of the pastoral team at the church I was attending and asked for help. She recommended that I reach out to a woman in our church who could disciple me. I had no idea what that meant, but I did it. Taking that first step was exactly as uncomfortable as you would imagine. The woman and I had common interests. She was the artsy type and since my degree was in Art History, the match seemed natural. However, calling a total stranger and asking her to disciple me was way outside of my comfort zone, but the fear of sliding back into the pit of discouragement I had just been lifted out of motivated me to push through.

> Taking that first step was exactly as uncomfortable as you would imagine.

One hard step, and then another, and another and I found myself at the end of an eight-week one-on-one discipleship season with Artsy. I learned that discipleship was just spending time with someone further along in their faith. She gave me her personal time in the safety of her home. She was a wife, a mom, and a faithful follower of Jesus. She was strong and full of courage; in fact, she had enough courage to lend as I took those hard steps.

She became a safe place for me to reveal my brokenness, patiently answering my seemingly endless questions. She didn't try to solve my problems for me, she didn't offer too much advice. Instead, she pointed me to my Bible for answers; she encouraged me to look to scripture for guidance and direction. Most importantly, she didn't whitewash a life with Jesus; there would be no shortcuts—over, under or around—the hard things that lay ahead for me. She was full of grace and truth.

Shortly after my time of discipleship ended, I met the man who would eventually become my husband and we embarked on life's adventure together. Hard was about to begin.

Now, twenty years down the road, I can attest that the years haven't been all sunshine and roses. I still have the journal I was using daily 10 years ago. And as I look through those pages, they transport me back to when we were navigating one of those hard times. A decade earlier, on the surface, it looked like we were launching into a wonderful season of life. Married with two beautiful children, a large home in the suburbs, nice cars, careers, and friends. To outsiders looking in, we had it all. The journal, however, reveals a different story.

> The seeds that were planted in me more so many years earlier, when I was new in my faith, had been neglected.

The seeds that were planted in me so many years earlier, when I was new in my faith, had been neglected. I hadn't given them water, or fertilizer, I hadn't cultivated the soil of my heart. Instead, I abandoned the process. My mentor's encouragement to seek and find the answers and guidance I needed from my Bible went unheeded. Yes, we were attending church regularly, but I hadn't fed my faith. My husband wasn't either. And because of that, all the wonderful milestones my husband and I achieved while building our life together had no foundation on which to rest. We had taken many shortcuts in building our life together. The façade was in-tact but the ground beneath us was weak. We were weak.

So often in the church, we hear messages about abundant life. Abundance means *full* or *more*, and so we naively assume that means, as Christians, life will be those things: life will be full. Life will be more than we have experienced to this point. We assume all this *more* will be pleasant. But the reality is quite the opposite. Jesus never promised that life would be free of struggle or challenges. When Jesus was teaching about abundant life to the people, He was telling them to listen to Him. *"If you do it My way, you will have life—both now and eternal—and you will have more than you do now."*

More.

As I reflect, I think that contributed to my downfall and ours. A misunderstanding of the "more." Once you have experienced the love and peace that life lived with Jesus brings you understand the true meaning of "more." It's never about chasing after material things or achievements. The world says the key to happiness is the pursuit of "more" in life. A pursuit which led me right back down into my pit of discouragement and brought my husband with me.

This is not uncommon when it comes to growing in our faith. I hadn't experienced enough growth to change my understanding. The life I wanted was more than the façade we had built; I wanted the real thing.

I wanted the house and cars without the huge hole of debt we had dug for ourselves by doing it the "world's" way. I wanted the careers without the stress that they put on our relationship – and our ability to parent our kids. I wanted our life to be filled with love and peace, not tension and anxiety. Coming to this place was a seed sown. And the recognition that we needed to change how we were living was another seed that would have to take root.

Instead of adding to our life like adding plants to our cart at the nursery. We needed to start with seeds. Growing things slow. Letting roots form, learning how to take care of ourselves, our relationship, and our blessings. And we did.

Thankfully, this time, I had some idea of the way up and out. Putting into practice what Artsy had taught me. Determined to nurture the seed of faith that had been planted in me more than

> Climbing out of the pit would be hard, but not impossible.

a decade earlier, I started with a daily prayer and scripture reading. It was a manageable little routine that fed my spirit and I watched as that little seed began to grow.

Climbing out of the pit would be hard, but not impossible. Not looking too far ahead, I focused on one day at a time. One step at a time. And with each step, I gained the strength and courage I needed for the next.

As a couple, we sought out wise counsel. Counsel we didn't have when we had made some of those initial choices. Yes, there were days we beat ourselves up. There were days when we wanted to quit, many days. Truth be told, I wasn't sure "we" would make it—it's hard enough to try to change on your own, throw another human in the mix and it becomes even harder! But that's where faith showed up for me and us.

Faith, like an invisible glue between us kept us, together. Imperfectly of course. I'm thankful that most of this change occurred behind closed doors. Frankly, it wasn't pretty. For the most part, transformation isn't attractive until it's complete. In the end, however, something beautiful bloomed. A marriage and home where love and peace found their place. Those are the untold stories that live in my tear-stained journals. The pleadings with God to help us up and out of the pit we had dug for ourselves. The written-out prayers. A record of the days I gave up hope in the moment—even the days I thought my husband had given up hope on me.

While I would have preferred another eight-week cycle of one-on-one discipleship or a three-step program to fix the messes that we had made in our life, walking through the pain—taking one step at a time through the hard—was the only way for us to experience lasting change.

We cut back, a lot! Downsized our expenses, our life, and even our calories. We did hard things. Made hard choices. Those hard things in life take time. Losing 50 pounds, paying off $50,000 of debt, pulling together a marriage that is hanging by a thread—they all required small consistent changes over time. And in between each tiny change, somehow God was helping us.

Yes, faith is like glue.

I've learned some valuable lessons in the years since I kept those journals. I know now that fits and starts, while not ideal, are very common in the life of faith. If you're in a season of needing to "start" again, don't be discouraged, just do today. Then do another day. And another. One step at a time. Every day offers a new opportunity to walk.

As I learned to walk with Jesus, it was never at a run; it was always one step at a time. When Jesus encourages you to take the hard way through—the way that requires you to persevere,

> It's the only way you'll learn that His way—while difficult—is the best way.

experience pain, get uncomfortable, wait, and face your fear—He's building you up; allowing you to grow your courage. He wants you to work through your mess instead of avoiding it. It's the only way you'll learn that His way—while difficult—is the best way.

Of course, as I was making the effort to grow in my faith, the weeds that had gotten me off course in the first place began to pop up again everywhere. Reminders of how weak I was, all those feelings of low self-esteem and low self-worth tried to choke my progress. I felt defeated some days and was tempted to throw in the towel more than once. But that little seed of faith growing with each tiny step of action was making me stronger, growing my courage. This allowed me to look inward and I began to recognize behaviors and patterns that needed changing. Living in the pit was no longer an option for me and I was growing what I needed to get out. The growth process needed to begin with me.

> For once and for all, I needed to believe that I was valuable. That I was worth fighting for.

The thoughts I had about myself, my worth, and what was most important for me to grow daily needed to come first. Oh, but it was hard. It felt selfish and stingy, but it was critical for me to re-define my self-worth. For once and for all, I needed to believe that I was valuable. That I was worth fighting for.

And I needed to remind myself of that often. So, I started weeding.

The daily encouragement in the scripture I was reading helped me understand that I needed to be able to take good care of myself. That I was, in fact, deserving of being treated with love and kindness. I was weeding out the lies I once believed and replacing them with God's truth about me. He created me, loved me, and had a good plan for me. And as those truths began to sink in, I started to treat myself accordingly. God was with me, not doing it for me, but steadily showing Himself through the process.

Little by little, over time, I gained strength, took a small step, and developed more courage. As incremental as it was, I was making progress. It was so encouraging. It showed up first in the way I cared for myself, which became evident in my physical appearance. Then, as my self-esteem grew, I became an emotionally healthier version of myself. Slowly, I began to see the change in my life.

As I grew stronger, it helped me to work through the messes that my husband and I had made together. We didn't take the easy route, nor did we find any shortcuts. The only way out was through. In hindsight, I can tell you that it required us to exercise enormous courage, and

> Mostly, by taking the hard way through, the way that requires courage.

it made us stronger as a couple. Both of us needed to learn how to grow our faith and allow it to change how we were building our life together. But if you had told me how many years of hard work it would take to undo the messes that I had made in my life, I don't know if I would have had the courage to do it.

Thankfully, I didn't have to do it alone.

The truth is, the woman I was a decade ago couldn't have worked through any of those messes without Jesus championing her every step of the way. It took years, but I didn't give up. Oh, believe me, I wanted to at times, but instead, I embraced the process. I did the work. And, now, ten years down the road, even though I still face struggles and challenges regularly, I'm living a full and "more" life—abundant life—with courage.

And you can too.

COURAGE IN ACTION: NEXT STEPS ON FAITH

Dear Discouraged,

I have volumes to say about faith. Not knowing where you are on your faith journey leaves me wondering how I can Champion you in the best way. I've shared just briefly parts of my own story—yet not the whole. However, for the sake of wanting to fulfill my promise to you—to be your Champion—I am including a Resource Chapter at the back of the book. I have compiled some action steps you might consider taking, depending on where you are on your journey. I've included some tools and organizations for you to consider reaching out to, as needed. If you're not quite sure if you're even on a journey, I have the next step for you as well. Remember, I am here to champion you along the way. You need to do the work, on step at a time.

I believe in you, Melissa

CHAPTER FIVE

*We can do anything we want to do if we
stick to it long enough.*

Helen Keller

Fear. Courage. Bravery.

These words are laced through the pins I've posted on my
"Inspirational Quotes" board on Pinterest. Why? Because fear
begs for inspiration, and courage and bravery embody it.

We all long to see courage in action. Humans, being created in
God's image, were designed for
greatness. Historically, we defined
greatness as the ability to achieve or
endure something that was both hard
and meaningful; however, this is no
longer the only narrative. We are living

> We are living in
> a generation
> that is obsessed
> with comfort
> and speed.

in a generation that is obsessed with comfort and speed. And
instant fame and fortune are possible to obtain. These dangerous
desires both carry tremendous influence without requiring
courage. And if a generation is feeding these desires by
shortcutting true greatness with the material, vain and
temporary, they will fall short—or shallow—of what we they
were made for. They will be insecure. And insecurity is a
breeding ground for fear.

Fear seems to be getting special attention these days. I first noticed this as I started looking more deeply into courage and all its various facets. One quote on my Pinterest board reads, *"Everything you ever wanted is on the other side of fear."* To me, this implies fear is a bad thing, an obstacle between you and the object of your desires. I'm sure the intention is to rally your inner girl-boss to action, to chase ambition, to be spectacular! But as someone who's already misunderstood God's way before, I wonder perhaps if that is misleading? Maybe there are two sides to fear. One that is designed for caution and another that points you in the direction of your God-given purpose? Maybe fear is the doorway to courage?

> Courage has a way of guiding our thoughts and actions toward doing what is right, and often hard.

If we look at our desires through the lens of courage instead of fear, what do we see?

Author, Maya Angelou, says this about courage: *"Courage is the most important of all the virtues because without courage you can't practice any other virtue consistently..."*

Courage has a way of guiding our thoughts and actions toward doing what is right, and often hard. It does this because it is a virtue. It knows no other way. And because of this, even if we fail along the way or don't prevail in the end, we feel secure. We know the pursuit was meaningful. The ultimate goal is to reach the place where your desire meets this side of fear. A fear that requires courage.

Maybe we need to be willing to believe that the fulfilling life we've always imagined is waiting for us on the other side of courage. That it is possible to see our desires fulfilled as we live out our purpose? That it is permissible to pursue our passion without the fear that it is wrong?

Imagine experiencing fulfillment free of fear but full of courage.

I believe that as you gain an understanding of courage and all of its attributes, you'll begin embracing this idea. I also believe this is the *more* Jesus was referring to.

I've chosen to personify Courage to help you identify with her as your strong female role model. You are like her already, you can allow her to influence your life, you can take on more of her identity. There are seven different attributes of courage that I will personify for you;

Courage chooses discomfort. She lengthens her stride beyond her comfort zone.

Courage perseveres in the face of adversity. She's no quitter.

Courage governs her fears. She knows them by name and knows she controls them.

Courage suffers with dignity. She patiently endures pain knowing that it has a purpose in life.

Courage fights for what is right. She defends herself and others against injustice.

Courage pursues her passions. She inspires others by living a fulfilling life.

Courage hopes. She values the process of waiting and uses time wisely.

Courage represents all that is beautiful and right, strong and steadfast, exciting and vivacious. She glides through the struggles of life with seemingly effortless grace. She's a head-turner for sure. Why then, are there so few who embrace her? I propose that shortcuts have played a large part in the population plunge.

Did you notice what was not on her list of attributes?

Here's what didn't make the cut: her clothing, her flat abs, what she is making for dinner, her lust to wander all over the globe. She isn't known for her professional financial prowess, how many letters serve as addenda to her name, her desk, or home décor. She doesn't pay any mind to her beauty regimen, where she shops, her latest diet fad, how Instagram-able her life is, how many likes did she get, or if she's going viral.

> Because, frankly, we all buy into the fears of the material, vain, and temporal daily.

I could continue the list for dramatic effect, but I won't. Because, frankly, we all buy into the fears of the material, vain, and temporal daily. I am no exception.

The things that didn't make the cut, they are not new to the scene of female distraction. They are, however, more readily accessible and more widely accepted pursuits than ever before. This is exactly why we must hold fast to the courage of previous generations, full of purpose, and not allow this contemporary imposter to take her place.

How do we accomplish this?

We need a perspective shift. We need to embrace that it is possible to live a life dedicated to cultivating the courage each one of us naturally possesses in our everyday ordinary lives AND be a 21stcentury woman.

Remember how I described myself way back in the Introduction? *A damsel in distress.* Well, I know now that was due to a lack of courage. Instead of using the little courage, I possessed, weeding my garden of discouragement, and watching it grow with

> I hadn't cultivated the seed of courage I naturally possessed and, as a result, I was desperate for encouragement.

each tiny act, I was begging God to do the work for me. To be my Champion and rescue me. I hadn't cultivated the seed of courage I naturally possessed and, as a result, I was desperate for encouragement.

I had also bought into the way of the 21stcentury imposter, short-cutting courage for comfortable and easy, and I was ill-prepared for the challenges, life was sending my way. But that was then, and this is now.

For me, what has filled the gap over time is a process that has included a succession of small actionable steps. One step at a time, learning to respond to the situations in my life through the lens of courage instead of fear. Putting into action the skills of each attribute that defines courage.

I was stuck in a pit of discouragement induced by my low self-esteem. The opportunity to speak up for myself presented itself over and over again in my everyday ordinary life, and I backed down every time. Full of insecurity. It wasn't until I made the courageous choice to take a small step of action, to use my voice, to speak up and defend myself, that I began to climb up and out of that pit.

There is a Chinese proverb that says, "A journey of a thousand miles begins with a single step." It doesn't matter how far you have to travel, taking one step at a time, looking at your obstacles through the lens of courage, and responding to life's challenges with the necessary attributes, most certainly will help you too. And I'm here to lend you a bit of my courage to get you started.

By now, you've probably got more questions than answers—that's normal and expected—but I suspect the most pressing questions might be these: Where do I even begin? Where do I lack courage? What weeds of discouragement do I need to pull? What series of steps do I need to take? Which path do I choose?

One way to answer these questions is by following a role model. Similar to personality profiles, models can help us see ourselves—and our behaviors—a little more objectively. They help us identify patterns. And in the way that real models for clothing and lifestyle show us what *could be*, pattern and behavior models do the same. They get us considering our patterns of thinking and behavior and reveal some of the weeds we need to be on the lookout for.

They also help us embrace the process of taking small steps: the small steps of identifying the weeds and beginning to uproot them. The small steps of cultivating courage in our everyday ordinary lives. The small steps of remembering—in the face of opposition—that what we are cultivating is a virtue.

> The small steps of remembering—in the face of opposition—that what we are cultivating is a virtue.

Are you ready to do the hard work?

I want to remind you, this is a process I've already been through, and so I promise to encourage you along the way by sharing my story. I told you way back in the Introduction that this was a book about me taking courageous baby steps in my everyday ordinary life and how that changed me as a person. I also said this *might* also be a book about *you* taking courageous baby steps in your everyday ordinary life to find out how you might change as a person.

Ultimately, the choice is yours. You have the choice to cultivate the seed of courage you naturally possess, to do some emotionally hard work, and to grow. Are you ready to make some changes? I believe in you. You can do this!

Let's look at the seven attributes that we've already outlined in a way that could help you identify an area where you consistently lack courage. I'm going to call these the *Courage Personas*. They are the *Stretch Persona, Perseverance Persona, Fearless Persona, Patience Persona, Advocate Persona, Inspiration Persona,* and *Hope Persona*. With each one, I will identify some potential weeds that might need to be pulled in the cultivating process. We're doing this one step at a time, as we consider the potential weeds.

Remember, the whole point of this book is to get you feeling a little uncomfortable; that's the seed of courage germinating within you. Your job right now is to allow it to grow. I want to encourage you to commit to proceeding, no matter how uncomfortable it gets, especially if your go-to ointment is typically shame, guilt, or introversion. The shame, the guilt, the withdrawal—those are weeds. Don't allow them to take root. Instead of letting them grow deeper, it's time to start pulling.

Stretch Persona: *She lengthens her stride beyond her comfort zone.*
Potential Weeds: Preferring that others downsize their lives to make you feel comfortable. Believing a small life is all that God intended for you, and everyone else. Refusing to show the people around you that you care about them by taking action with them in the things where they experience delight and fulfillment because you will be uncomfortable.

Perseverance Persona: *She's no quitter.*

Potential Weeds: Believing you're the only one who's ever had it tough. Refusing to take the initiative—especially where an apology or admission that you did not give your best effort is concerned. Waiting to start and/or continue until conditions are optimal for your success. Indulging in self-pity and empathy to the point of inaction.

Fearless Persona: *She has tamed her fears.*

Potential Weeds: Using your fear to control and manipulate others for your comfort. Wearing your fear as a badge of honor. Taking pride in labeling your fear and committing to live in it as a means to avoid change or growth.

Patience Persona: *She understands pain has a purpose.*

Potential Weeds: Denying that you are in pain and need help and/or that you have used a short cut—like self-medicating—to avoid experiencing your pain. Skipping processes which are designed to bring about a purpose from the pain. Habitually taking short cuts and developing a "one and done" way of living.

Advocate Persona: *She's a skilled fighter.*

Potential Weeds: Fear of conflict. Fear of breaking rules. We live in a society governed by rules, roles, and responsibilities. But those things can easily become crutches we lean on to avoid stepping into a problem that's not ours. That fear is a weed trying to choke our humanitarian responsibility and civic duty. Here's a test: if it was happening to you, would you hope for someone to step in?

Inspiration Persona: *Her passion is attractive.*
Potential Weeds: If you are stuck in the habit of pursuing fulfillment by *getting* something *from* the world instead of being fulfilled by *producing* something *for* the world—you have a weed that needs pulling. You were created to make and do and throw off seeds when you mature. When you are not living with purpose, you will most certainly become discouraged.

Hope Persona: *She knows how to wait.*
Potential Weeds: Complaining. If you struggle with patience, what that means is that you can't suffer—or be uncomfortable—without complaining. Vocalizing your suffering constantly will give it more territory in the soil of your life. Just as waiting is hard for everyone, so is suffering.

Did you catch my Persona? The Advocate Persona. This is the attribute that I hadn't cultivated in my youth. Make no mistake, the Advocate knows how to roar. Over time, with small actionable steps, I cultivated this attribute as well. Now it's your turn.

Which Persona did you relate with the least?

Perhaps reading through these personas has opened your eyes to some weeds that have taken root in your own life? Perhaps you're stuck in a pit of discouragement and you need a hand up and out? Perhaps you need someone to lend you some courage while you start the hard work of pulling your weeds? Of learning to be your own Champion? Of believing that you are worth the effort?

I believe you can embody as many of these attributes as you desire. I believe you have a tiny seed of courage within you and that you are destined for greatness if you're willing to do the work. I believe in you. Do you?

As we lean in to grow and change and better ourselves—to take on the characteristics of these personas—it's important to remember that we are just seedlings. In the beginning, we'll be delicate. As we tend the tiny shoots of courage growing within us, we need to be kind and gentle to ourselves.

But as we continue this process of cultivation, we will slowly but surely become women of courage.

Women who stretch beyond their comfort zones.
Women who never quit.
Women who refuse to live in fear.
Women who suffer with dignity.
Women who fight for what is right.
Women who inspire others.
Women who always hope.

You have that potential within you.

And that, my friend, is Pin-worthy.

COURAGE IN ACTION: NEXT STEPS ON GROWTH

Dear Discouraged,

My role as your Champion is to encourage you. To lend you a bit of the strength I've gained by taking this journey ahead of you. I do this by sharing some of the hard of my own story. My difficulty with conflict resonates with the "Advocate Persona." This was an area of my courage that was under-developed. But this isn't the only area where I've struggled.

Let's you and I consider "Fearless Persona" together. The reality is that we all have fears that are very real. And there is always a temptation to make the excuse, "But Melissa, you don't know my story!" And you're right, I don't. But I'm committed to helping you by sharing mine.

I have a fear of falling. This fear is deeply rooted in trust or lack thereof. While I was growing up, the adults in my life were either unable or unwilling to provide the necessary safety and security I needed. This pattern began when I was a young child and continued throughout my youth. The result of that became an irrational fear of falling from great heights and every time I got high off the ground, this fear was triggered. It's rooted in insecurity.

Over time, and with some hard work, I came to realize that my trust in a very critical relationship in my life was broken early on. This caused my

71

mind to associate a physical fall with the emotional fall I experienced as a child. Here's the thing that I know now, believing that my fear of falling is warning me of potential future harm, is believing a lie. That fear is a fake, a liar, an imposter. I have named it and tamed it and locked it in a cage.

Yes, triggers like to unlock that cage, but I don't allow the fear to come out and mess with me anymore. If I hadn't done the hard work of discovering the "why" behind this fear I would have missed some amazing experiences, like a helicopter ride over the Haleakalā volcano in Maui on my honeymoon, riding the elevator to the top of the Eiffel Tower or climbing the stairs to view the Sistine Chapel.

Here's another example of real fear. I have had several very bad car collisions; ones with damage so bad, it's a miracle they weren't life-threatening. Several occurred in inclement weather—specifically on icy and or snow-covered roadways. Ask anyone who knows me how much I like riding in a car in poor conditions—even rain. They'll tell you I only need to be in the car to squirm, I don't even have to be the driver.

Sometimes, to get through a ride, I need to close my eyes, or I choose the false safety of the back seat to endure my pain.

And that's what it is, a fear of potential pain. Just like my fear of falling, the fear of potential pain is anchored in my physical experiences. It's the real deal. But, still, I get in the car. I refuse to give in to a false reality my fear wants to create, which entices me to feel unsafe.

The truth is, we have no idea what our future holds and there are a million things we can't manipulate or control. That's why living requires courage. Engaging fully in your everyday ordinary life is a sure way to cultivate it. There's more ground to cover. So, I ask you to search down deep into the soil of your soul and ask yourself some brave questions. Look for some potential weeds.

Which Persona do you relate with the most?

The Courage Personas can help us identify areas where we can grow our courage. Part of developing any skill is through practice and training. Learning what to do and what not to do are fundamental in skill-building; these are ways we develop good form and habits. The same can be said for developing our courage. That's why I'm excited to share a resource I created for you: The Courage Persona Quiz. This quiz can help you self-identify which Persona you may be strongest in as well as identifying areas where you need some encouragement. The site where you find the quiz is listed in the Resource Chapter of the book. This tool can help you put what you've learned into practice. It is my gift to you.

I believe in you, Melissa

CHAPTER SIX

Courage starts with showing up and letting

ourselves be seen.

Brené Brown

It was right about year ten in my marriage—during the season when I realized my faith needed some serious nurturing—when I found my community.

I had dabbled a bit in serving at my church before, but this was completely new to me. I don't know how it happened exactly, but in short order I found myself joining the women's leadership circle.

Maybe it was their desperate need to put a warm body in the classroom, or maybe it was my fresh enthusiasm about all I was learning and had still to learn, about God. Whatever the reason, it was the path God chose. What I do know for sure is this: I had never seen a community of women like this one. Like lions on the Savannah, they were their own pride. And, as the newest and youngest member of the pride, I had a lot to learn.

> Whatever the reason, it was the path God chose.

Given the instability of my upbringing, I wasn't given much attention; therefore, as a learner, I am a master of figure-it-out, learn as you go, and ask questions, which is hard. It is for exactly this reason that I'm attracted to the very opposite; to clear instruction and the stability of seasoned leadership. And this faith community had both. I was content to keep my mouth shut and my eyes and ears open.

The routine of the leadership circle was not identical, but similar, to the rhythm of my weekly Bible study group. We opened with songs and prayers, discussed our answers to the questions in the lesson, and closed with more prayer and some chit chat. The one significant difference was that this new circle was full of leaders—that is, strong women.

I hate it when people use the term "alpha" to describe someone's personality, warping and twisting strength into social dominance. Strength is strength. And, in women, in particular, it should be viewed as a

> Strength is strength. And, in women, in particular, it should be viewed as a beautiful thing, not necessarily a "male" thing.

beautiful thing, not necessarily a "male" thing. Leaders, regardless of whether they are male or female, need to be strong. They carry the weight of influence, not social importance. And, in this new environment, I was about to get a lesson on strength.

She wore it so well.

Both her wig and her cancer. So much so, that I was part of the leadership circle for several weeks before I was even aware of the weight she was carrying. It can be a heavy burden when the world needs us to be all smiles on the outside when we feel like crying on the inside.

But within our leadership circle, there was no need to cater to the needs of the world; the pride was there for her. Most weeks she'd have a smile for us but, occasionally, we'd find her crouched in her chair at the end of the hymn we'd been singing, or the prayer we'd been praying, silently weeping into the palms of her hands. It was clear to me that within the confines of our group, she felt safe. And, indeed, she was fundamental in creating that feeling of safety.

Her role within our community was to welcome the newcomers and care for the needs of those already in our study—it was a job she did beautifully, making people feel at home, creating a sense of belonging. And, as I watched the way our members responded to her, I learned some valuable lessons about servant leadership. My peers came alongside their sister, bore her burden when it was too heavy, and patiently paused until she found her footing again. They endured her pain and waited with her through her suffering.

I was watching and learning firsthand about the cycle of courage in the community. They lent her the seed of their courage when she simply had none of her own. She borrowed the strength they offered through their encouragement. And when

> I was watching and learning firsthand about the cycle of courage in the community.

she was ready, she would contribute by scattering some of her own when someone else needed it.

The truth is, life's hard. All of us can find ourselves knocked down at one time or another for one reason or another. But, time and again, I've seen the difference between those who get back up and those who don't is the ability to borrow the strength of others when they need it.

Similarly, we all need a safe place to express our fears and the opportunity to borrow the courage we need to face them without judgment. I learned this when my new friend from the circle confided in me one day. She shared with me about a hard season in her past, I found myself having to work to simply receive her perspective, and not justify it or judge her because of it. She was openly sharing, assuming that I was present to listen. This was new to me. It was a lesson on vulnerability that I needed to learn.

I was raised in an environment that was obsessed with judging others and that was my default. However, it quickly became apparent to me that if I was going to be able to handle this kind of intimacy, I had some work to do.

When I learned to remove the lens of judgment, an amazing thing happened: I was able to see more of who my friend was, the fears she faced, and how she moved through them to become the person I was now befriending. If I had judged her because of the things she shared with me, I would have missed some great lessons. I also would have pushed away an important friendship.

Have you heard the phrase, "Girls compete but women empower"? It was exactly this situation and being part of the pride that taught me the truth about this statement. As this woman shared her fears with me, how she faced them, and what she was enjoying on the other side, she was doing just that— empowering me. She was imparting all kinds of lessons on strength and courage and overcoming fears, using the fragility of her own life to teach me.

In much the same way, I observed other members of the pride interacting with one another in this way. Sometimes, it looked like a bit of a dance, other times it was gentle wrestling. It was evident they were not in

> She was imparting all kinds of lessons on strength and courage and overcoming fears, using the fragility of her own life to teach me.

competition with one another, but—instead—being vulnerable, being open to listening to a perspective different from their own, setting boundaries while still helping others realize their full potential.

Ah, yes, boundaries.

This was another important lesson I learned in the pride.

Society is comprised of boundaries—if not physical or structural, such as buildings, walls, and fences—then social and emotional, such as etiquette, familiarity, and appropriate social distance. We don't generally hug someone we've just met. If you're ordering a coffee, the barista usually stays on the other side of the counter. Some things are acceptable and some are not.

Women in community are no exception. In our leadership circle, if you spoke out of turn, or went too far off script, you'd be told in not so many words. But directness in the female community is not always well-received or tolerated. A firm, "Hey, I'm not okay with that" can be misinterpreted as aggression and it can easily illicit unexpected waterworks, which might be misconstrued as weakness. But, when there are no structural boundaries to respect, we need to use our words. Watching the strong women in my leadership circle navigate each other's boundaries while defending their own was interesting and occasionally intimidating.

I was doing my best to observe the ladies in action, learning what was allowable and what wasn't, catching the social cues along the way. When, one day, it became apparent that a line had been crossed. I still vividly recall where I was seated in the circle of chairs that day. The most senior leader among us was a few chairs to my left. Her challenger was a few chairs to my right. I was center court for the action that would be unfolding.

From the beginning of our time together that morning there had been friction in the air. Knowing that conflict was a weakness for me, I was an uncomfortable witness to the interaction between them. I don't remember the words they exchanged, but I was overwrought with the thought that such conflict would be part of the culture of this community I had grown to love and cherish. True to my nature, everything in me wanted to run.

I didn't learn until much later that these behaviors are all very similar to those found in a pride of lions. Playful wrestling, establishing boundaries, a roar to confront a potential threat. These things are common within communities of strength. But most notably, lions don't engage from a place of fear, but from a place of courage; there is no hissing or scratching allowed.

I needed to embrace that the benefit of the lessons to be learned from the pride could not be gleaned without enduring the rigors of its social dynamic. It was in witnessing the healthy way these women navigated their conflict that I finally came to accept that running away could no longer be an option for me. The encouragement they provided and the strength of their example were the very things I had been longing for. It would only be within the tension of female relationships that I would be transformed. It was by watching and learning from these strong women that I discovered that by using my own voice and my own words to set my boundaries, I could stand firm in the face of conflict. They were teaching me how to roar.

Sadly, I didn't know at the time that my place within that pride would be temporary and I would soon have ample opportunity to practice what I had observed.

My weekly Bible study meeting, which had proved to be a lifeline for me, was one necessity I would need in my new life after we moved. My husband and I had uprooted our family and followed our dreams to a different state thousands of miles away. Shortly after we moved, I looked for a local Bible study to join. My previous experience had taught me it was a safe place to build relationships, keep me anchored in my faith, and experience community in this new place.

It was never my intent to get back into the leadership circle, I just needed a place to feel welcome. But somehow, I found myself called into service once again. So, naturally, I assumed the experience would be similar to my previous group. Again, I shouldn't have assumed.

Within this new leadership group, I found out the hard way that there's a huge difference between watching others assert their position within the pride and doing it myself. It became very clear to me that, this time, I would be participating in the playful wrestling and confronting roars. I would need to summon my courage.

> I would need to summon my courage.

Call it what you will—hard, awkward, painful—confrontation is rarely pleasant. And my inexperience in this area was about to be put to the test. I would need to pull from all those lessons I had recently learned about strength, vulnerability, and setting boundaries.

I asked a lot of questions. I wasn't challenging her, I was trying to learn, but I don't think she saw things that way. She had a witty charm I admired, but, in dealing with her own life transitions, she was under pressure. She wasn't even sure she could fulfill her obligation to the group without having to deal with what she likely perceived as my newcomer's neediness. Witty was carrying a heavy load. If nothing else, my questioning had become an irritation.

In an unguarded moment, Witty revealed this irritation toward me cloaked in a bit of sarcasm. I felt it immediately; it hurt. It cut like the swift swat of a claw. In no way did I receive it as friendly. But most of all, it hurt because she was the matriarch of my new circle.

I had to make the hard choice to be vulnerable and tell her that her words hurt me. I needed to do it solely for the sake of not running away from the community I desperately needed. And with the resolve to practice changing my behavior and my response to conflict, I communicated to her that it wasn't kind. I knew my confrontation was not likely to produce a perfect outcome, but I had to take one small awkward step in the way of practicing.

> I had to make the hard choice to be vulnerable and tell her that her words hurt me.

I didn't know exactly how the interaction would play out. However, I considered it a good thing that she was older, wiser, and more seasoned than I, and I trusted she would handle my objection with grace. It might not be easy. It may not be with pleasure, but I was confident it would be with the controlled strength of a leader.

And so, it was here where, instead of watching courtside, I experienced my first engagement in the circle. And, for the most part, because she handled it with such grace, I came away unharmed. With much hesitation, I shared how her remark had made me feel. And to my relief, she apologized immediately. I knew she had regretted her words because she followed up the apology with a request for a new beginning.

> It's the paradox that holds the answer. The very attribute of courage that is hardest for you to express is the same one that can be the most transformative.

She expressed the desire for the exchange to be a gateway into a stronger bond of relationship. A learning opportunity. Which it was. In the end, I was more courageous, stronger because of it. That's one of the great things about courage: it grows as you use it, a little bit at a time.

This was another lesson that I needed to learn; one that deserves to be shared with you.

It's the paradox that holds the answer. The very attribute of courage that is hardest for you to express is the same one that can be the most transformative. And once you dare to take your first awkward step to exercise the courage you need, in the area that needs the most development, you are likely on your way to becoming a more extraordinary you. The hero of your own story. A Champion.

For me, it was facing the tension of conflict with other women and learning to come to my defense. Learning to use my voice to speak up for not only others but also myself. If this resonates with you, then I hope you've gained some encouragement from my story. Yes, the tentative first steps will be hard, probably painfully so. And yet, as I've proved, not impossible.

Or, you may be attracted to one of the other Personas from the last chapter. You might be feeling challenged by the potential of where your courage needs growing and seeing where you have weeds that need to be pulled. Either way, I can't help but feel excited for you as you position yourself to grow. The beauty is this: the process is always the same. One-step and then another.

> The beauty is this: the process is always the same. One-step and then another.

First, learning that you can grow your courage right from the everyday ordinary experiences in your life. Then, becoming, more and more, the strong and virtuous woman God created you to be—an extraordinary woman.

COURAGE IN ACTION: NEXT STEPS IN COMMUNITY

Dear Discouraged,

Right about now you might be in one of two places: either you have found your place within a healthy and supportive community of woman or you are hurting because I've just touched on something you know you need. Depending on where you find yourself, I have some next steps to offer you. If you've got your people, I say "Yes! So happy for you." If you don't, I want to make an appeal. Be brave!

You can see I had to try multiple times to develop the courage I needed to experience that kind of community in my life. It took too long. Don't wait. You need female relationships. And while I can't have coffee with you in person, I don't want to leave you hanging. Please see the Resource Chapter of the book for ways to connect with me and other women. If you've tried before and had a bad experience, I get it, please try again.

I believe in you, Melissa

PART THREE

Progress not perfection.

CHAPTER SEVEN

You gain strength, courage, and confidence by every experience in which you really stop to look fear in the face. You must do the thing which you think you cannot do.

Eleanor Roosevelt

It took me far too long to realize that I had been waiting for permission.

Which is especially absurd on the heels of the small victory I had experienced with Witty. But this was still new to me and I was a novice. It was my own permission—or lack thereof—that was the very thing holding me back from taking action. That was it. And there would be no moving out of the old identity of powerless victim that I had worn for so long until I was brave enough to give myself permission. Permission to use my voice, to speak up for myself, and to set some boundaries.

Deep down inside I needed to continue to pull on that same weed. The weed that supported the message that I wasn't worth it. The weed that said that it was somehow wrong to come to my own defense. The weed that insisted on permission.

At some point, I just needed to believe that I not only had the

> At some point, I just needed to believe that I not only had the right to define my boundaries, but I also had the right to defend them.

right to define my boundaries, but I also had the right to defend them. It was up to me to define what was acceptable and what was not in the way people spoke to and acted towards me. It was up to me to draw my lines in the sand.

I also needed to be okay with the knowledge that the further out I set those boundaries, the more likely I would be rubbing up against other people. That had to be a risk I was willing to take; rubbing someone the wrong way.

People like to have their egos stroked. So, when someone tells you that they didn't like something you said or something you did, it rubs, like coarse sandpaper against rough-hewn wood. I think this is one reason women have such a difficult time navigating the fence line of boundaries. They don't like the friction.

Generally, women tend toward people-pleasing. We don't like hurt feelings and we don't like to hurt others. Of course, there are always exceptions, but we tend to be sensitive to ourselves and each other. You might even say that sensitivity is our superpower. The trick is to not allow ourselves to be overly sensitive to the point that we can't handle any rubbing. This becomes evident when we need to set boundaries. Navigating this fine line requires great skill.

The same sensitivity we need to consider the feelings of others is also the way in which we protect and guard ourselves. And this can become especially complicated within female relationships. Without even realizing it, an overly sensitive woman can sow weeds in her sister's garden instead of encouragement.

Insecurity spreads like the cotton-topped bloom of a dandelion gone to seed. With the first puff of breeze, seeds will float on the air multiplying the choking effect of the mature yellow flower it will soon again produce. When an insecure woman takes her sensitivity with her—leaving unresolved differences in her previous relationships behind—and sets off to forge new ones, she becomes a weed sower.

I certainly did not want to sow weeds. I desperately wanted to pull them. That's where I needed to begin. I needed to begin to sow my own encouragement. Permission granted.

And with that, I slowly put into practice what I learned to become my own Champion. God was shaping a new identity in me. Emboldened by the courage I was growing in small steps, I resolved to turn my attention toward the conflict and hurt I had experienced with Sassy in the kitchen incident.

It was a good thing that I had tested the waters with someone seasoned enough to recognize that my approach was birthed out of vulnerability and a desire to bond, and not break, the relationship. In this situation, I was far less certain of how things would play out when I decided to voice my feelings to her. My intuition told me this would be complicated.

> If I avoided the pain in front of me, I was sure it would rear its ugly head in the future.

Although I was dreading what I knew lay ahead for me—that is, communicating my feelings to Sassy—it was entirely unavoidable. I simply could not run the risk that my silence could be interpreted as approval. This one hard conversation with her would ensure no additional opportunities to feel small and insignificant in my own home ever again. If I avoided the pain in front of me, I was sure it would rear its ugly head in the future. It was now or never.

It had been a few weeks since the kitchen incident. There had been no interaction in the interim. Life had continued at a rigorous pace for our busy families. But for me, the black hole of silence was as if time had stopped and waited for me to process and pray through my response. And just like the locker room in middle school, the only thing that interrupted that silence was the deafening sound of my beating heart as I picked up the phone to dial her number.

I knew there would be no way to make my words perfect. But after a few exchanges back and forth, small talk and the like, I just had to spit it out. Which is exactly what I did. Here's how I remember it: "I need to tell you that I wasn't okay with you deciding that you were going to give a speech at my house, at an event I planned, for my husband."

You can imagine my words were not received well. There was immediate tension. She was in the safety of her own home, the only thing connecting us was the miracle of cellular technology. Her countenance must have shifted as her ears absorbed my message. A few seconds of silence later she responded.

"I don't know what to say other than I feel very uncomfortable."

My directness, it seems, had pierced her the same way hers had pierced me that night in my kitchen. I had now instigated the very same journey her actions had brought upon me. Sassy would now be faced with calling upon her courage. She would need time to find it.

Quickly, she expressed that she preferred to end our conversation and did not see spending time together, neither ourselves nor our families, as something she had a desire to continue to do. And within moments the phone call ended. It would now be my actions that created a ripple in several relationships becoming a sore spot for months. As much as I wish that things may have been handled better or more skillfully on my end, there are no guarantees that the relationship would have weathered the exchange differently. I had to find a way to let my mistakes go. I needed to accept that progress was more important than perfection. I was a novice, a learner. And learners only gain proficiency through practice. The habit of dealing with and expressing myself needed to become permanent before I would gain skill and tact.

I had to permit myself to take a step.

We all need to permit ourselves to fumble our way through in the beginning.

Here's where all of our stories intersect. The same God who didn't swoop in and make the way easy for me, the one who walked with me through the difficulty knowing that with each hard step He was building me up—making me strong and steady like Him—is the same God who let *Sassy* experience discomfort. He allowed it so *she* could walk with Him and pull her weeds of discouragement and tend her soil. He's the same God for *you* too.

He doesn't want you living like a damsel in distress, He wants you to be the extraordinary woman He created you to be. Full of courage. He's helping you to learn how to grow it in the circumstances of your everyday ordinary life. He knows which area of your courage needs development, and He wants you to use the courage you have to grow even more.

Because you need more if you're going to give it away, lend it out, and encourage others. You need to be full of it, for yourself and the people around you. That is what He made you to do: He made you to be an encourager.

And that's what He made Sassy do too.

But for the time being, we would need to learn these lessons in different circles.

After the many months that we were both growing and changing as women in our own right, we would find ourselves mutually surprised when our roads to progress would find their way ending in the same place. Life, if nothing else, is full of surprises. Some excite us and fill our souls with expectation and wonder. Some flood us with shock.

This would be one of those shocking moments.

I was looking forward to a new opportunity to grow and stretch and apply what I had been learning during the distance in our relationship. I had been invited into a new circle of sorts, one that would, again, thrust me into a level of serving that would challenge and develop me. That was until I saw Sassy's name registered on the list for the Bible study I would be leading. I wasn't looking for that kind of challenge. I can't imagine she was either.

But here's where we found ourselves once again. There was nothing I could do but just move forward and see what would come about as we re-engaged with one another. I sent an email out to everyone who would be attending the Bible study, her included. That was the catalyst for Sassy's call.

She had received my email, and being caught off guard, was probing for clarity. I explained that I would be leading the Bible study she had registered to attend. Once there was an understanding, we were left with that heavy silence that accompanies disjointed conversation: the awkward pause. But courage prevailed, and we agreed that maybe it was time to sit down over a cup of coffee wearing our big girl panties, and till the soil a bit to see what might be planted.

There we sat across from one another, coffees in hand. Sassy made the first move. "I'm sorry that your feelings were hurt." There would be no need to make unnecessary introductions as to what she was referring to—we were both well aware of the elephant who had decided to have coffee with us that afternoon. I noticed with dismay that she managed to acknowledge my hurt without assuming any responsibility for the injury. It was the same finesse with which she sauntered. And although I wanted her to own her actions in the same way in which I received them—as overstepping and careless—I wasn't willing to rehash what would most likely result in an unreconcilable difference of opinion. So, I let her words suffice.

> Because this was never about an apology, this was about me taking a step of courage.

Because this was never about an apology, this was about me taking a step of courage. To use my voice and stand up for myself. To break through the invisible barrier of permission and to take action. To cultivate the extra to my ordinary. Each of us had taken a step and I decided that's what was important.

We left coffee that day with new freedom girding our relationship. At least for now, the shock of occupying the same circle in the future would no longer be enough to push either of us away.

We all bring some level of insecurity into our relationships. Over time it's the acceptance we receive in safe places that disarms this insecurity and allows those weeds to wither. The rhythm of give and take, lend and borrow, these things keep our relationships in balance. When you enter with no courage of your own, you disrupt the natural cycle that keeps relationships alive.

I've witnessed this too often, relationships that have been broken by weeds that insist on taking root and chocking out healthy interaction. Especially in circles of women. That's why we all need to have some encouragement to bring with us into the community. Because as women, this is what we're created for, to build these circles. Circles that heal and mend, love and give, provide safety from the broken world we live in. We need to create and contribute to communities strong enough to strengthen each other and help each other along.

For me and Sassy, mending what had been broken was an important step in the process. And at the right time, I would appreciate that all along, she and I were each to play a part in God's good plan.

CHAPTER EIGHT

Stand for something or you will fall for anything. Today's mighty oak is yesterday's nut that held its ground.

Rosa Parks

Only months after the mend, a friend of mine who owns a small book printing and publishing company offered to give me some boxes of books. And, although my husband would have preferred that I offload some of my stash (which was at risk of taking over our garage), I said yes. I knew there were several volumes of homeschooling curriculum that were quite expensive in the boxes, so I was happy to share the loot with my homeschooling friends. The extra books were a bonus.

There were scads of books that had been printed mostly for distribution to friends and family: recipe books, short devotional books, and written accounts of God's faithfulness. But buried deep within the rubble of feelings and sentiments I found a book that captured my attention, *A Big Life*, by Peter Hone. [i]

Who doesn't want a big life? I don't think there are too many people who—when asked—would answer that they'd prefer a small, unfulfilling life. But never learning to take courageous baby steps in our lives can very quickly set us on that trajectory.

Without a Champion to show you the ropes early on, you can begin living small before you know it.

Learning to live big as an adult can be even harder. The habit of changing a mindset, putting it into action, and distributing your own high fives can be a daunting task, and I had found myself in the thick of it. Intrigued, I pulled that title out

> Without a Champion to show you the ropes early on, you can begin living small before you know it.

of the cardboard graveyard from where it was buried, gave the dust jacket a good puff, and dove in.

The stories were riveting, graphic, and inspiring. They stirred in my imagination things that could re-light the fire of my faith. By this time, I had been walking with Jesus for two decades. I had seen my husband come to faith as well as both of my children. I had (begrudgingly) laid down my career for family, committed to the hard call of being a homeschool mom, and had served as a lay leader in several discipleship ministries. But I had to admit, my faith needed some fertilizer.

When we get to the place where we are constantly drawing from the past in a weak attempt to encourage and motivate ourselves, we're no longer growing. We've stopped cultivating. And even though we all need seasons of rest, rest is not a destination; it is simply a moment in the journey that allows our soil to replenish its nutrients so the next crop can grow.

I was coming to the end of a season of rest and it was becoming clear to me that I needed a new challenge. The book was exactly the right message for me at that moment. I was ready to cultivate more courage for the journey ahead; God

> And even though we all need seasons of rest, rest is not a destination; it is simply a moment in the journey that allows our soil to replenish its nutrients so the next crop can grow.

already knew. And, as I lay in bed with my husband a few nights later, finishing the last few pages of that epic tale, I closed the back cover and I spoke it out loud, *"I want to go to India."*

When I said those words, I wasn't hoping to satisfy my travel bug. They spoke to my thirst to grow, to serve, and to cultivate my courage in a new way. That's what a "mission" trip is for, it gets you to "do" something. And just in case you've missed the point I've tried to make along the way, doing and growing go hand in hand.

Make no mistake, there are a million baby steps one must take between *saying* they want to go to India and actually going. Each step would serve to cultivate the courage I would need to take the next step, which would eventually get me there. Requiring me to exercise other aspects of my courage. It would be hard work, but I was ready.

I'm not sure, if either of us had known, whether we would have committed to the trip. But somehow, by God's divine

103

orchestration, we found ourselves sliding onto the same vinyl bench seat in the church's cargo van, me and Sassy.

In total, there were nine of us traveling together, all women! We were a motley crew, for sure: all ages, colors, and sizes. And, for the most part, we would only share three things in common for the next eleven days: our femininity, Jesus, and India. She and I—on the other hand—had a colorful history to add to the mix. There we were, sharing a seat, about to test the strength of the trust bridge we had recently rebuilt.

It takes courage to let old things die so new things can grow. Had I not spent time pulling out those weeds of low self-esteem to make space for what God wanted to do in my life, I would have never been able to survive that trip. To be clear, there were opportunities at every turn for me to be hurt and offended and ample opportunity for discouragement. But I had learned to be my own Champion and employ the skill of self-encouragement. I learned how to fertilize the good and pluck out the bad before it had a chance to fester. No toxic roots would be allowed in my garden. And because I had learned to cultivate my courage, I was available to encourage my trip mates when they needed it the most, even Sassy.

We hadn't even reached the airport before she began to share: She was discouraged. Her boss was giving her a hard time and her husband, for his own reasons, wasn't exactly thrilled that she had decided to go on this trip. When the voices that carry weight in our lives don't encourage us, we can get discouraged. This is especially true when we're accustomed to having their support.

So, there she was, already discouraged; it was not a good way to start the journey. God was bringing us to the other side of the world to encourage women, but it was clear we needed to establish our own culture of encouragement to support and sustain our circle. I didn't realize it at the time, but for those eleven days, we would need to become a pride. As Sassy and I sat together in the van, it occurred to me that it was time for me to share what God had been teaching me. Not only for the women we would be serving, but also for the women I would be serving with.

I'm a planner. Give me a list and I will check all the items off and then some. Packing for my trip to India was no exception. By all accounts I was over-prepared, with ankle-length cotton skirts for every day of the week, mini-flashlights, packaged snack foods, and—knowing we'd be visiting during the rainy season—some fabulous animal-print galoshes and raincoat to match. I was ready for anything, or so I thought.

It turns out that readiness isn't about the equipment we have, it's about the person we are. I *was* prepared and ready for that trip, but it was the journey leading up to boarding the airplane, not what I had packed in my suitcase, that made the difference. It was all the baby steps I needed to take along the way—the paperwork, the prayer, the meetings, the

> It turns out that readiness isn't about the equipment we have, it's about the person we are.

research, the fundraising, even the travel immunizations—that prepared me for what was to come. Each step was a tiny exercise in courage, strengthening that muscle.

Here's what I've since learned about being prepared. There is no way to anticipate everything that will happen in life. We can do everything in our power to mitigate disaster, but life will throw us curve balls. And curve balls will sometimes require us to have courage.

It was day one and the morning prayer call broke the silence of darkness early. The curtains were drawn, and I lay there stiffened in my bed as my eyes searched about for orientation. We had arrived very late the prior evening and in the flurry of arrival, I hadn't noticed the mosque situated near our hotel. As suddenly as I woke, I realized that I was finally here! My journey towards courage had brought me here to this extraordinary place. It was exhilarating!

After a quick breakfast that was the Indian expression of Western fare, we left the comforts of the bustling 21st century city slowly by bus. It was as though we were traveling back through time to a place where running water and power aren't guaranteed. It would be there in that dusty village in India where she and I would reconnect and be reminded of the strength it takes to be a woman, still even today, in every corner of the earth.

There was an odd mix of contemporary civilization peppered throughout the rural landscape. Mopeds zipping by horse-drawn carts filled with farming tools. As our air-conditioned, airport-style shuttle bus drove by, I saw a woman wrapped in ornately dyed cotton down to her shoeless feet walk past the gas station, a large pitcher carefully balanced on her head. Seemingly incompatible time periods peacefully coexist in this place. Dirt roads connect concrete communities where white dust and exposed rebar are common. The village children run to greet us with smiles for miles. Their white teeth contrasted with such dark complexions. They are beautiful.

The organization we were traveling with had invested in the lives of the women of this tiny remote village. And on this day, we would have the great honor and privilege of distributing graduation certificates for those who had participated in a life skills development program in sewing. Their excitement over our attendance was palpable and we were humbled to be there.

At the lunch break, our group sat chatting together in a circle seated on white plastic chairs—the ones that create a suction to the back of your legs on a hot summer's day. The topics ranged from what we were to eat, when would we be leaving the village and where should we relieve ourselves. All eyes looked at our trip leader for answers. In response to the last of those queries, she laughed, "If I was you, I'd hold it. There is no way I'm going while I'm here." This was her advisement to the group. However, we'd spent the morning in this same room with the climate of a sauna and it had given me a thirst to match. The copious amounts of water I had consumed was running its natural course and holding it wasn't a choice to be made. Thankfully, I wouldn't be the only one who needed the relief.

And so, Sassy and I stood up to face whatever was waiting for us in the bathroom together. By this time in the planning and trip, we had managed to break through the ice of awkwardness, sitting next to each other on the transfers and even rooming together in a hotel. It was a good thing because we were both about to have an opportunity to take some courageous baby steps together.

After a bit of hand gesturing and with the help of an interpreter, a lovely woman from the village escorted us to the facilities. Knowing there was no running water in the village, I had prepared myself for an outdoorsy type of solution to our problem. But, much to my surprise, she began to lead us through a series of tiny rooms near the back of the brightly painted concrete building where we had spent the last several hours. When we reached the last room, our guide stopped and motioned toward something. It was quite dark, and it took my eyes a few moments to adjust to the dimly lit space. A small window high up on the side concrete wall let a tiny beam of light cascade into the space.

My companion and I looked at each other, both of our faces marked by confusion.

With spoken language being a barrier between the three of us, we wondered if something was amiss until our guide made some motions. At that moment, all the differences between us faded into nothing, and everything that unified us rose to the surface.

We didn't need to speak the native tongue to understand what she was communicating.

Our escort motioned toward a dark corner of the tiny room and as we shuffled our feet a little closer in the direction she pointed, I could just make out a lip that boxed out the corner of the floor, similar to a shower pan. Sitting on the floor nearby was its companion element, a five-gallon bucket, filled with water that you could use to "flush." This was quite different than the outdoorsy facilities I had envisioned.

> At that moment, all the differences between us faded into nothing, and everything that unified us rose to the surface. We didn't need to speak the native tongue to understand what she was communicating.

After looking my trip-mate square in the eye, there was only one question that needed answering: who would go first? I was leaning toward action but since I was still having trouble seeing the target I deferred to my companion, who somehow had the foresight to wear her galoshes despite the brutally hot, dry weather that day. It was at that moment that I wished I had worn mine. We were told to wear layers of conservative clothing, so the act of gathering it all up so we could do our business was a bit of work. But, worrying about protecting my feet wasn't something that had occurred to me before this moment.

"I'll hold your hand while you go, and I'll hand you a wet wipe," I told my companion, knowing full well that a wet wipe wasn't going to make this situation any better.

She expressed her stage fright once she had found her way into a good position, needing to be careful not to miss the mark. I tried to be encouraging. There we were, the three of us—yes, our escort was still present—doing what women do all the time; after all, we're known for going to the bathroom in groups. But this was intimacy on a whole new level!

After a time, I handed Sassy the wet wipe, and silently embarked on my private pep talk, thinking again how helpful my galoshes would have been at this juncture. Thankful for all the jogging I had done for the past several months, I was just able to squat deep enough to avoid my shoes. Our escort held her hand out to help me balance while my companion re-adjusted her layers of garb. I can only imagine how the lady from the village would retell this interaction to her circle of friends; I'm sure we had made an impression on her with our wet wipes and all.

Then, just when I thought it couldn't get any more awkward, a cell phone broke the silence of our shared awkward moment.

> Only in India can you be in a remote village with no running water or electricity, and still have a cellular phone! Crazy! Tucked in the bosom of your sari, no less.

Yes, a cell phone. Effortlessly, our guide changed the hand she was holding mine with and reached into the bosom of her sari to access her phone. Only in India can you be in a remote village with no running water or electricity, and still have a cellular phone! Crazy! Tucked in the bosom of your sari, no less.

My trip mate and I were speechless, but we shouldn't have been. Women have behaved this way for generations—we are the ultimate multi-taskers. I was grateful that our escort continued to hold my hand even while she took her phone call, because the truth is, I needed her strength to help steady me. Likewise, I was thankful that my trip mate hadn't chosen to abandon me there in the dark, with an unfamiliar hand holding mine. Even though we had some history, we still had a relationship. I knew I wasn't alone.

Once we were finished, our escort motioned us away and reached for the nearby bucket. How humbling it was for us that she would serve us in this way. She may not have spoken any words to us that day, but her steady presence set a profound example and encouraged us in our journeys. As we walked back through the maze of concrete rooms, reuniting with our team, all there was to do was laugh. Moments like this one remind me of what it means to be a woman: the mix of intimacy and vulnerability combined with strength and purpose. These are the complex ingredients that connect us so deeply and help us to become courageous.

> Moments like this one remind me of what it means to be a woman: the mix of intimacy and vulnerability combined with strength and purpose. These are the complex ingredients that connect us so deeply and help us to become courageous.

Throughout the rest of the trip, there were many more moments that stretched us all. Collectively, our group shared dreams, experienced breakthroughs, and fulfilled a lifetime of longings. For me, it was a courageous step into the big life I felt God had destined for me. This trip was a milestone on my journey, not just because I had to cultivate the courage necessary to go, but because I had to learn how to continue my growth when I returned home. If I

> And, I wanted more than a single experience, I wanted lasting change.

couldn't carry the experience back with me and let it impact my life in a meaningful way, then it would become just that, an experience. And, I wanted more than a single experience, I wanted lasting change.

Those eleven days provided me the time and space to think, and dream, and hope about how I could take the ordinary, everyday moments waiting for me at home and turn them into opportunities to cultivate an extraordinary, courageous life.

I have a pocket full of cherished memories from my trip to India. Memories of air so thick and filled with spice that you could almost cut through it. Memories of smiling faces, naan of every variety, and monkeys. Memories saturated in vibrant color, seasoned with curry and chai, filled with fabrics, and baskets, and painted cows. But perhaps none of them match the memory of our good-bye.

After a long and tiring trip home, one marked with delayed flights and the impatience of a group of weary travelers, it was our final goodbye that marked the end of our years of uncomfortable interaction. We re-convened at the baggage carousel after greeting our loved ones with enthusiasm that belied our fatigue. Years had gone by since the kitchen incident, and though we hadn't brought it with us on the trip, it still had a place in our everyday ordinary lives back home.

It was at that moment that we had a decision to make, we could choose to bring the healing of our new, shared experience with us, or we could choose to leave all that was sown during that trip in India. The choice was ours. As we retrieved our luggage from the baggage carousel, we would be left with no more reason to delay our next inevitable step. We needed closure. We needed to write the end of our story.

I decided I wasn't going to miss the opportunity and I took a baby step in Sassy's direction and watched her turn toward me in response. With her shoulder slightly turned in my direction, I leaned in for a hug, not out of obligation, but by choice. And as the embrace loosened and we pulled away ever so slightly from one another, a look passed between us. A look and expression that marked the journey of courage we had both traveled together. A journey of two women who were once wounded but were now healed. A journey where we had learned to accept and appreciate one another. A journey where we learned to love one another, just as we are called to do.

CHAPTER NINE

One day or day one. You decide.

Unknown

In just the same manner as I turned toward her, I am now turning toward you, friend.

What will be your courageous story? Courage invites us all to be

> Courage invites us all to be transformed.

transformed. Perhaps, my story of healing the pain of my low self-esteem has intimately touched you? Or one of the Courage Personas resonated with you? Our courageous baby steps will likely look different, but the journey we will take is essentially the same.

The question is: are you ready to take the journey?

Have you considered the steps you need to take to move into a more extraordinary version of you? What are the opportunities available in your everyday ordinary life that will help you transform into the hero you desire to be? A Champion. Can you identify potential experiences where you can purposefully choose discomfort? Learn to persevere? Face your fear? Allow your pain to serve a purpose? Begin to pursue your passion? Or maybe even be brave enough to wait, yet still holding onto your hope?

If you're still reading, I'd venture to guess that you've answered an emphatic "yes!" You are ready to take the journey, one step at a time.

It makes no difference if you were drawn to this book or whether the book found you; what matters is that you can't shake that feeling you have right now. The feeling that you, too, could be living a bigger life—a life that requires more courage.

You can take steps up and out of your pit of discouragement today.

You don't have to continue feeling unfulfilled by your complacent life, the extraordinary life you've always imagined is waiting for you is just on the other side of a succession of courageous steps forward.

Are you willing to risk that this might be a book about *you* taking those steps? That's what I'm hoping I've encouraged you to do: start by taking one step.

In Chapter One I shared my steps with you.

Step One had to do with self-awareness. Being courageous enough to accept that where I was—both my mindset and my perspective—was not in alignment with the vision of the person I wanted to be. These things were also inconsistent with who I believed God wanted me to be; a woman whom He designed to be strong and courageous, a woman full of virtue.

Step Two was identifying patterns of cowardly behavior. It was time to arm myself with some tools for tending the soil of my soul. It took a lot of reflection on my part. I needed to examine the areas of my life where my actions lacked integrity. The areas where my thoughts and feelings—the things that make me who I am—were not lining up with the things I was doing. And I needed to measure these things against the grace and truth found in God's word.

My feelings, thoughts, and actions make up my soul—my little kingdom. When they are going in different directions, I lack integrity. It's okay to acknowledge our lack of integrity, in fact, I believe it's healthy, as long as we can be both kind and encouraging to ourselves as we do it.

This is miracle-grow for the soil of your soul. Accepting both the hard realizations of where we are and the potential of where we could grow to be. Friend, these are the things that make good soil in your life.

Step Three involved stepping up and then stepping out. This is the sweet spot of learning to become your own Champion. You can learn to become your own cheerleader by giving yourself small actionable steps and then doing them. It doesn't have to be hard or dull; you can make it fun, even if you don't have an Achiever personality. Once you identify the areas of courage you

> Once you identify the areas of courage you need to cultivate you need to step up to the challenge and step out in action.

need to cultivate you need to step up to the challenge and step out in action.

About seven years ago I got all caught up in the social community of slogging. That means, I became a slow jogger. I was not a runner, because runners compete; sloggers participate. This simply means if I signed up to be in a race, no matter the distance, I didn't expect to see my name on the list of top finishers. In these types of races, medals aren't reserved for the winners, everyone receives a participant medal. If I finished, I was a winner!

It was here, despite my lack of interest *in both jogging and competing, where somehow,* I found myself pulled into the South Florida phenomenon that is social racing. Trust me, if you kept your eyes open on any given day where I live, chances are you'd come across at least three people wearing participant race shirts. We all own them.

This sport was good for me for a while because it was a way for me to get some good cardio in regularly and it's not very expensive. However, after several races I noticed something about myself: I was dumping the race medals in a drawer in my closet. My friend, on the other hand, has a display for hers in the foyer of her home. They do not hold the same value for me as they do her. And, after some consideration, I realized I had done the same with my college diploma certificate, which was framed, as well as some other post-grad recognitions I had received. Every achievement was hidden from plain sight! Why?

The more I thought about it, the more I realized I simply didn't care. I cared more about *doing* it than being recognized for doing it. That was important for me to understand about myself. Being recognized for what I was doing was not an effective reward system for me. The medals, awards, and recognition weren't a motivator like they are for people with Achiever personalities. I just needed the growth that the opportunity and the challenge provided. The lesson here is, if you're going to become your own Champion you will need to know what motivates you.

With each weed you identify and pull you need to have a reward for yourself; a way to acknowledge that what you are doing is worth applauding! Because it is. Growing yourself, having the courage to improve and change and become the best you that you can be is most definitely worth applauding. So be ready.

While I may not be an achiever, what I have learned is that I am a doer. And doers love nothing more than to get things done. For me, that includes keeping a personal development plan for myself. One that considers actions I can take to grow. While I may not want to become a working chef, I am interested to learn new cooking techniques. I may want to take an art class or read twenty books in a year. None of these things will get me awards, but all will develop me as a person. And, in the end, I get to say I completed what I set out to do. I get the pleasure of knowing I did something important to me. All of which were worthy endeavors and fun! Finding your motivator is key!

> Finding your motivator is key!

Getting this right leads to a more fulfilled you. And we are all looking to feel more fulfilled.

Identifying which area of your courage needs growing, and then following this three-step process will get you started on your journey.

In Chapter Five, I rolled out the red carpet for Courage in all her glory and sophistication. You may need to go back and review a bit. Take some time to thoroughly consider if there is an area of your courage that could use a little weeding and strengthening. You might also benefit from some real, practical tips on ways to do so. Especially if you find yourself feeling complacent and bored with your everyday ordinary life, practical steps can serve as a boot camp of sorts. Refer to the Resource Chapter for those.

> Be brave, take a step. God's given you enough courage to ask for help.

What I didn't mention in Chapter 5 is if you've found yourself locked in a cage with your fears or are having a difficult time processing your pain, you may have fallen into a pattern of denial or deep despair. If this is the case, your first step of courage might be to ask for help. Real help from people who are trained with tools and resources that are designed to support your efforts to climb up and out. You need a community around you that understands how steep your climb is. It's possible that just to even begin, you might need more than encouragement.

Be brave, take a step. God's given you enough courage to ask for help. I've included some places to ask for help in the Resource Chapter.

But what about the need for a community? A circle? A pride of your own?

If you're reading this and thinking to yourself, *"What about me? I'm in my pit of discouragement and I don't have a circle to run to."* I don't want to leave you there, friend. I'm here to help.

Oh, how I wish I could offer you the one-on-one attention I received early on in my journey from the strong and courageous woman at my church. I'd sit with you face to face, nestled in the quiet security of my home. However, this is not possible.

What I can do is scatter the seed of encouragement in your direction and invite you into a circle that does the same. I'd like to invite you into a pride—if you will—a circle of women committed to encouraging and supporting one another in a vibrant, online community I've created for exactly this purpose.

Again, please see the Resource Chapter provided at the back of the book. This is where you will find all the instructions you need to join us.

If this message I've shared about cultivating courage out of the everyday ordinary opportunities of your life has you all fired up and you've got "all the feels" over it. Maybe, your next step is to spread it? Become a fangirl and take up the mantle of Champion and build your own circle, establish your own pride. If this is you, one way you can encourage me is to let me know. I've included my contact info on the last page, send me an update on how you are moving this message forward with your people and I can share some additional resources to equip you.

> It's time to start living your own courageous story.

For all of us, myself included, the most important thing is that we don't settle and say, "That's all nice and good, but I don't need any more courage." Because that is a lie! The world desperately needs extra-ordinary women holding up every pillar of society and that requires us to all become our most courageous selves. It's time to start living your own courageous story. You are a Champion. The world needs your roar.

Dear Discouraged,

Now is the time for your own beautiful story of transformation to unfold. Take steps to leave your pit of discouragement, became your own Champion. This, of course, is a journey. A journey toward courage.

You have this courage within you.

Yes, it may be buried down deep inside you, but I'm sure it's there. And that is the key to unlocking your own transformation story. You need to find your courage and grow it. It's the simple truth about courage. You can't buy it, or make it, or inherit it, but with the borrowed seed of encouragement, it can be nurtured. You can learn to grow it!

Learning this lesson didn't come easy and putting it into action was even harder. But that's what made this a story about transformation. My transformation. But what about your story? Are you ready to start your journey? I hope so. Your story is waiting.

I believe in you, Melissa

Acknowledgements

To Sassy, Artsy, and Witty – just a few of the women who God used to transform me, I say "thank you." I am blessed by the support of my family and friends. And without the partnership of my copy editor, Janine, with Janine Dilger Creative. I'm not sure I would have reached the finish line without her services. Thank you all for taking the journey with me and seeing me through to the other side.

RESOURCES

COURAGE IN ACTION: NEXT STEPS ON FAITH

In Chapter Four, I shared the very beginnings of my faith journey, my simple little prayer, which offers you a glimpse of what I believe. Here is a more complete picture: I am a Christian. This means I believe that our good and perfect God, the Creator of everything, wants to have a relationship with me, and every human who has been conceived since the beginning of time. But He can't. Because humans are not perfect like He is, I'm not perfect and neither are you.

This is a problem. The Good News is that God solved this problem for us. Out of love and His desire to have this relationship with us. He became human. A perfect human. And His human name is Jesus. This may be confusing if you've heard something like; God the Father, God the Son, and God the Holy Spirit (or Ghost—which is definitely confusing). Those "names" are just a way of explaining God in the three ways He exists.

As a Creator, He is very much like a father.
As a perfect human, He existed as Jesus.
As a Spirit, He lives in Christians.

This "living in" is how we experience Him in a relationship. This is a very basic explanation of something inexplicable, so please bear with me. Similarly, the way I've outlined that courage grows through action you become a Christian by action.

My little prayer was the action.

All I needed to do is believe that Jesus was God and a man who lived a perfect life. He died for my imperfection, (which is also called "sin") then came back to life three days later. I know this for two reasons: the first being that witnesses saw Him, and those accounts are recorded in the Bible and because God gives me the faith to believe what I didn't get to see with my own eyes. Jesus left His human form forty days later and told those witnesses He would return. No one knows when.

We are still waiting.

Yet, miraculously, people still believe this message when it is shared. It is alive. That's how we have a relationship with someone who we cannot see. God's Spirit is with us. And we are promised that Jesus will return, and we will be with Him forever, restored to the perfection God created in the beginning. That is what a Christian believes. Now, here's the action that requires courage.

Do you believe?

If you've never taken your first step on this faith journey here's my special invitation to you. Email me. Send an email to Melissa@MelissaCDyer.com and in the subject line type: FIRST STEP OF FAITH. In the email, I'd like you to share your questions and I will respond.

If you are a Christian and are struggling with fits and starts in your faith here are a few steps, you can take.

- Reach out to another woman you know who is further along in her faith journey than you are. This was my first step. I needed someone who could give me some coaching! A good starting point might be asking your church pastors for a recommendation.
- Commit to attending church weekly, reading your Bible and praying daily, keeping a journal of what you learn.
- Listen to Christian radio. You can get the same music you hear at church on the radio. I remember how I felt when I was very new in my faith when I discovered this! "Why hadn't anyone told me?"
- Muster the courage to get outside of your comfort zone and join other women who are growing in their faith. They are right there in plain view, you just have to look in the right place. You'll find them in your church and women's Bible study groups.
- Over time, develop your own spiritual growth plan. This can include memorizing scripture, serving at your church or another organization. Planning and taking action are what you can do to keep moving forward.

There are many ways to grow in your faith, this is just a beginning. Don't be discouraged if you've taken these steps before and you feel like you're stuck and wondering if your journey has stopped. Your courageous step is to begin again. Just take one step and then another. That's the only way to get unstuck.

COURAGE IN ACTION: NEXT STEPS ON GROWTH

In Chapter Five I asked you to consider this question; Which Persona do you relate with the most? As I laid out "Potential Weeds' for each Persona you may have an idea of where you need to grow your courage the most. And since we've already established that the way to grow your courage is through action here a few tips to practice.

Stretch Persona: *She lengthens her stride beyond her comfort zone.*
DO: Take advantage of opportunities to try new things. Make it a lifestyle. All you have to do is try. Here are some everyday ordinary life examples: new foods, activities, and meeting new people. You don't have to love it, or even like it, but you do have to try it – at least once. And, even if the experience is less than awesome, you still need to continue to try new things regularly.

DON'T: Say NO to something unknown or new just because it might make you feel uncomfortable. Saying NO often makes your life shrink. If you find yourself refusing to try new foods, activities, or getting out of the house to meet new people, your courage will atrophy.

Perseverance Persona: *She's no quitter.*
DO: Make "finish what you start" a personal mantra. After all, victory goes to the finisher, not the starter. Carefully embark on projects and goals with a commitment to finish well. It's not a competition, however competing occasionally will help you grow this kind of courage with flair, as will accountability and creating a reward system for yourself. There is also the need to exercise vulnerability here; especially where relationships are

concerned. Calling for back-up by way of coaching, counseling, or any other form of help when you want to quit is a success habit, not a weakness.

DON'T: Blame your circumstances. Circumstances will always assert themselves against your commitments. This headwind affects everyone. Don't make excuses. If you decided to start, it's your responsibility to finish. Doing your part *is* your part.

Fearless Persona: *She has tamed her fears.*
DO: Know what you are afraid of and why. Name your fears and learn to tame them. Ask yourself questions that reveal how irrational your fears are and re-write the hypothetical outcomes. Know the triggers that unlock the cages you've built to contain your fears. Take action regularly in areas that trigger these fears to emerge, so you can transform your taming practice into a mental habit that closes the cage quickly.

DON'T: Get inside the cage with your fears. Don't meditate on the things you are afraid of and make justifications for their hold over you. Don't make excuses to avoid confronting your fears. Don't let pride keep you from asking for help in the "name and tame" process. Don't project your fear onto others.

Patience Persona: *She understands pain has a purpose.*
DO: Maintain an emotionally healthy perspective. Consider all of the natural processes in life that are full of pain but exist for a purpose: seeds die to become trees and a woman gets pregnant only to endure birth. Suffering is a natural process in life. The trick is to make good use of your suffering. When you need to wait for someone or something—including you—before you

131

can move forward, focus your time and energy on what you can do, not what you can't.

Journal. Keep records of these seasons to remind yourself that they are just that—a temporary stop, not a destination.

Be thankful for the process. If not absorbed over a long period of time, most pain would overwhelm us either physically or emotionally. Processing over time allows pain to become bearable.

DON'T: Avoid pain. Medicating or numbing so much that you can't feel or process your pain weakens your natural capacity for endurance. This includes chemical medication, substance medication, food, retail, and relational ointments we use to minimize, cover, and numb us to pain. If you've experienced trauma, proceed with the help of a medical professional.

Advocate Persona: *She's a skilled fighter.*
DO: Use your voice. Words are just as powerful as fists. Learn to use them well and you can bring about change, build bridges, or save lives. Like all skills, it takes work and practice to learn how to use our words well. All beginnings are awkward and clumsy, but if you push through and practice, you'll soon learn how to defend your boundaries as well as come to the defense of others who have no voice.

DON'T: Be silent. If no one stands up for what is right, wrong prevails. Don't assume it is someone else's responsibility to be an advocate. If you are aware that your voice is needed in a particular situation, you don't need permission to step in and help out. Don't let fear stop you from doing the right thing. Even a clumsy advocate is better than no advocate at all.

Inspiration Persona: *Her passion is attractive.*
DO: Pursue what you love. Of all the seven attributes, this is the one that sparkles. God made the world to be beautiful. And, as one of His creations, that includes you. Pursuing your passions helps you to stay beautiful. Your passions add color, fragrance, and ornamentation to your everyday ordinary life. Whether it's art, or craft, or sport, doing what you love brings you to life and makes you attractive to others. Everyone is looking for inspiration, you could be the one who inspires. As you do the things you love, you're also honoring the way God made you. And that's beautiful in itself.

DON'T: Believe it's wasteful or frivolous to pursue what you enjoy. Don't believe the lie that your circumstances need to change, that you need more money, more time, more space, more talent, and so on. All you need to do is commit to beginning. Start small but do start.

Hope Persona: *She knows how to wait.*
DO: Know the difference between waiting and procrastinating. There is a difference. Waiting means, you either don't know all that you need to before moving forward or you've done your part, and time must reveal the rest. Waiting is being obedient to what you know is the best, even if you don't understand why. Waiting will wear your faith thin but strengthen it in the process. Waiting will challenge your hopes and dreams and put you to the test.

DON'T: Think that circumstances will eventually change, and things will be easier. The truth is simple: Waiting is just hard. Don't blame outside forces, don't make arbitrary deadlines, just wait.

These are just potential action steps you can take. You know yourself better than anyone else, find what will work for you and commit. The accumulation of small steps in the same direction is the journey.

Another resource I mentioned in Chapter Five was The Courage Persona Quiz. This quiz can help you self-identify which Persona you may be strongest in as well as identifying areas where you need some encouragement.

Visit www.MelissaCDyer.com and take the Quiz today!

COURAGE IN ACTION: NEXT STEPS IN COMMUNITY

Finding your pride, a community of strong women who can encourage and support you, is a necessity. I shared how finding these women changed my life. Here are three organizations that are populated with these women: that offer solid and sound teaching and are populated with like-minded women interested in growing in their faith.

Community Bible Study: communitybiblestudy.org
Bible Study Fellowship: bsfinternational.org
Precept Ministries International: precept.org

Now, I'm not saying the only way to find strong women is to look for them in a Bible study, but this is where I first found a group of these women. And a community is a group. I have lots of friendships but there is something special that happens when we are gathered together in a group. Encouragement within a community is an experience you don't want to miss out on. Alternatively, if for some reason you are unable to step into a group where you have face to face contact regularly for encouragement, there is another option.

I have created an online space where women can get together to encourage each other. This in no way replaces the benefits of in-person gatherings but is an invitation I want to extend to you. This is a private Facebook Group and you can join by visiting my website www.MelissaCDyer.com, look for the words "GROW IT."

However, I mentioned if you've found yourself locked in a cage with your fears or are having a difficult time processing your pain, you may have fallen into a pattern of denial or deep despair. If this is the case, your first step of courage might be to ask for help. Real help from people who are trained with tools and resources that are designed to support your efforts to climb up and out. You need a community around you that understands how steep your climb is. It's possible that just to even begin, you might need more than encouragement.

Be brave, take a step. God's given you enough courage to ask for help. But you need to ask in the right place. This is when you need a counselor or therapist. Here some places to find professional help:

PsychologyToday.com-use the "Get Help" tab to find a therapist or support group.

BetterHelp.com-can help match you with a therapist.

AACC.net-The American Association of Christian Counselors website offers resources and a database of professionals you can search.

And finally, if you're a Champion already and want to share this message with other women, I'd love to know. You can sow some encouragement my way by connecting with me on social media, see the Author Page for details.

DISCUSSION GUIDE

1.) The Author shared her journey of overcoming the fear to speak-up for herself and how that helped her live with more courage. Based on the title of the book, were you surprised that this was the journey she needed to take? How was that journey transformational?

2.) Is this an area of struggle for you? How was the Author's personal journey helpful or inspiring to you?

3.) Once you were illuminated to the "Courage Personas," was it easy for you to self-identify with at least one area where you are courageous?

4.) Did the "Courage Personas" help you see an area where you need to cultivate some more courage?

5.) Have you taken the Courage Persona QUIZ? Did you agree with the results?

6.) The Author is making the case to develop your courage in all areas; so that you are not held back from living your fullest life due to one area of weakness. Do you agree with that argument?

Why? Or why not?

7.) How where you able to relate to the Author's perspective and interpretation of what courage is and what it isn't?

8.) In what ways do you agree that courage can be cultivated in the everyday ordinary moments of life? How has this book helped you believe this to be true?

9.) Give an example of where you're able to relate to the Author's journey of becoming her own Champion?

10.) Why do you think women struggle with low self-esteem and discouragement?

11.) What motivated or and inspired you the most to take an action step that builds you up as you use your courage?

12.) Write down one step you might take today that requires courage. If you're comfortable, share this step with a friend. Take turns championing one another on your move towards growth.

ENDNOTE

i Hone, P., & Heerema, J. (2011). *A big life: Ordinary people led by an extraordinary God*. Mustang, OK : Tate Publishing & Enterprizes.

About the Author

Melissa C. Dyer is a writer, wife, mom, and Champion of women. *Learning to Roar* is her first book and passion project. She lives in sunny South Florida with her family. You can keep up with her other writings and content by visiting her website or connecting with her on social media.

www.MelissaCDyer.com
https://www.facebook.com/MelissaDyerWriter
https://www.instagram.com/melissacdyer_

Made in the USA
Columbia, SC
02 September 2020